JANE LUNZER GIFFORD

Published in 2007 by Murdoch Books Pty Limited
www.murdochbooks.com.au

Murdoch Books Australia
Pier 8/9, 23 Hickson Road
Millers Point NSW 2000
Phone: +61 (0) 2 8220 2000
Fax: +61 (0) 2 8220 2558

Murdoch Books UK Limited
Erico House, 6th Floor
93–99 Upper Richmond Road
Putney, London SW15 2TG
Phone: +44 (0) 20 8785 5995
Fax: +44 (0) 20 8785 5985

Chief Executive: Juliet Rogers
Publishing Director: Kay Scarlett

Project manager: Jacqueline Blanchard
Editor: Paul McNally
Design concept: Vivien Valk
Designer: Heather Menzies
Production: Adele Troeger
Photographer: Jane Lunzer Gifford

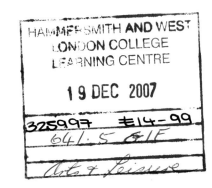

National Library of Australia Cataloguing-in-Publication Data
Lunzer Gifford, Jane.
Pret A Manger: food on the move.
Includes index.
ISBN 9781921208911.
ISBN 1 921208 91 0.
1. Pret A Manger (Firm). 2. Convenience foods. 3. Quick and easy cookery.
I. Title. 642.1

Printed by Midas Printing (Asia) Ltd in 2007. PRINTED IN CHINA.

CONVERSION GUIDE: You may find cooking times vary depending on the oven you are using. For fan-forced ovens, as a general rule, set the oven temperature to 20°C (35°F) lower than indicated in the recipe. We have used 15 ml (3 teaspoon) tablespoon measures. If you are using a 20 ml (4 teaspoon) tablespoon, for most recipes the difference will not be noticeable. However, for recipes using baking powder, gelatine, bicarbonate of soda (baking soda), small amounts of flour and cornflour (cornstarch), take away a teaspoon for each tablespoon specified.

CONTENTS

"It's like ham and eggs:
the chicken is involved,
the pig is committed."

MARTINA NAVRATILOVA

FOREWORD

Congratulations, you've bought a Pret recipe book. It's been exactly twenty years in the making.

We receive endless requests for our recipes. It seems downright selfish not to share them (and more). In this book you'll find inspiration and reliable instructions on how to make wholesome, natural, preservative-free food that is colourful, delicious and not too tricky.

There is no secret to Pret's success. The truth is, Pret's quite simple. (It's also unique.) We use good ingredients (we abhor the weird chemicals used in so much modern food). We create recipes that are straightforward and classic. We make and sell fresh food (we'd never buy from sandwich and salad factories). What we don't sell we give away to charity.

Lastly (and most importantly) our staff are proud, hard-working and extremely professional. They are the heart and soul (and make and break) of our shops and recipes.

If you know and love Pret, thank you.

If you've never eaten with us, please give us a try.

In either case, over the next few pages you'll find more vital information about the Pret crusade.

JULIAN METCALFE, PRET FOUNDER

HOME TRUTHS, MENUS AND STUFF

★

"Tell me and I'll forget. Show me and I'll remember. Involve me and I'll understand."

CHINESE PROVERB

In many of the world's cities you'll find places pretending to be Pret but missing it. The characteristics which make Pret unique are hard to copy.

Pret operates a bit like a restaurant. Every Pret has its own kitchen (except for one or two of the tiny ones). You won't find 'sell by' dates on our fresh sandwiches and salads. We don't sell 'factory' stuff. We offer our food to charity at the end of each day rather than keep it over.

We shun the obscure chemicals, additives and preservatives common to so much 'prepared' and 'fast' food. Our ingredients are delivered fresh every day. We don't mind that fresh and fragile ingredients go off quickly — we start from scratch each morning.

We buy free range or the equivalent. When possible we buy organic. We do this because natural fresh food tastes better than processed food and it's good for you.

"A fanatic — one who won't change his mind, and can't change the subject."

WINSTON CHURCHILL

Apparently we (that's you) want cheaper and cheaper food from our supermarkets. We think this is nonsense.

How come the price of a fresh chicken has come down over the last ten years? How can a whole bird be bought for only £2.20? What are they doing to it?

Food manufacturers aren't liars — they just leave things a bit grey (sometimes). Trans fats, weird bulking agents, strange oils, yield-enhancing drugs and preserving potions, not to mention bucketloads of sugar, are dumped in our food these days.

Low fat chemical food is all the rage. Don't you think 'low calorie' chocolate cake is ridiculous? It's not the answer. It tastes bad and is dumb. If you want to be slim then eat good quality, proper food in moderation and avoid processed junk and snacks.

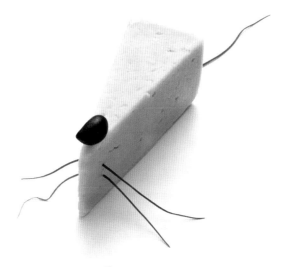

Over the years Pret's menu has become much lighter. More salads, Slim Pret sandwiches, No Breads, miso soup and light soups. Pret is living proof that eating healthy, delicious food is very possible. Our chefs have created some good dressings and sandwich sauces using yoghurt. We put butter in only two (out of thirty-six) of our sandwiches.

As for the environment, we'll continue to do our best. More biodegradable materials are in the Pret pipeline. Our 'bio-box', cornstarch pots and recycled bags are going down well.

We're buying more electric vans and we'll continue to support charities all over England with free food and money (last year we gave away about a quarter of a million pounds worth of food and cash).

Annoyingly, some of our food goes in the bin because there's no means to get it to the hostels. If you run a charity in need of good food let us know.

Pret is growing (one shop at a time, no rush). If you're hard-working, enjoy good food and have a sense of humour, do get in touch on our website.

Our training academy, communications department and environmental support team so often need good people. Likewise our 'non-suits' at our 'non-suits head office' are promoted and developed from within the company. We do tons of training, get in touch.

"Give a man a fish and you will feed him for a day. Teach a man to fish and you will feed him for a lifetime."

CHINESE PROVERB

Because we're a (smallish) private company we're not under pressure to grow. One day we'd like to make 9% profit. Maybe we will, who knows?

Pret doesn't want to franchise, so please don't call us and ask for a franchise because we don't. We really don't. We don't like to franchise so we don't.

PLEASE GIVE US YOUR HELP ON A COUPLE OF THINGS

We commission the Bond Street jeweller, Tiffany & Co, to make solid silver stars for us.

Whenever a kind word comes in about a member of a Pret team, off goes a silver star. Thank you to every customer who has been so thoughtful as to contact us.

We're always looking for new, delicious, natural ingredients. Do you have a friend or neighbour who makes something that you think would be great at Pret? Anything from jam to sausages? Please let us know or get them to call us.

We react to your feelings and ideas (the good, the bad and the ugly) with haste and sincerity. Please email us, or call me or our MD Clive Schlee; he hasn't got much to do … hassle him!

If you're a Pret customer, you have the right to be listened to.

We will continue to pursue harmony and balance in the business of making and serving great food. We'll continue to do what we can to respect the welfare of our customers and hard-working, wonderful staff.

The quote that follows is a bit out of place, but it's a winner. If Pret were a TV show (and sometimes I wish we were) we'd be *Monty Python* over *Big Brother* ... any day.

"The idols of today are unmistakable
— self-esteem without effort,
fame without achievement,
sex without consequences,
wealth without responsibility,
pleasure without struggle and
experience without commitment."

RABBI DR JONATHAN SACKS, JANUARY 2004

Thank you for buying our freshly prepared, good, natural food.

PRET A MANGER, 2007

FRESH FOOD ON THE MOVE

At Pret, nothing is made to last, apart from our principles. Our chefs start from scratch very early in the morning to make 'fast' food for you to take away; it's fresh food to eat on the move, anywhere and at any time.

Good-quality, fresh, natural ingredients are the basis of everything we do at Pret. The recipes we create (or tweak) evolve in our kitchen at Hudson's Place. The ideas start with the Creative Chef; he works with the Head of Food and Development Chef until they all feel able to audition the salad, sandwich, cake or bar at a Food Meeting. If accepted, the new model is life-tested (over a number of hours, alone in the fridge), has its wrapping and labelling developed and exhibited to the Food Team (the cat-walk) and is launched in our test shops (hoping to be noticed). If it sells really well, it is added to the Pret list and heads for the wider world.

This book gives you the recipes for many of the favourites that have made it to the top, so that you can make them at home. We have also added other recipes: serious contenders that are really at their best only when just made, some that are high maintenance and impractical on the high street, and hot treats that need to be handled with respect.

The sandwiches, salads and Pret pots are all made in our individual shop kitchens. Cakes, bars, smoothies, snacks and sushi are made for us, to our strict recipes and standards, and delivered daily to our shops. The recipes have to work extremely well so that there is consistency in quality and flavour. We are very picky about the size and shape of all our ingredients and make silly demands of our staff to be sure that everything is uniformly measured, sliced, mixed, assembled and wrapped.

WHAT DO WE DO?

To repeat an over-used phrase, sandwich making is not rocket-science and, having glanced through the recipes in this book, it might seem remarkably unimpressive when you become aware of what is obviously a pretty straightforward approach. After all, we could simply have told you:

$$2 \text{ x bread slices} + 20 \text{ g } (^3/_4 \text{ oz}) \text{ mayo}$$
$$+ 50 \text{ g } (1^3/_4 \text{ oz}) \text{ protein} + \text{seasoning}$$
$$+ 4 \text{ slices of veg} + \text{salad leaves}$$
$$= 1 \text{ perfect sandwich.}$$

We could send you on your way, wondering why it is that we can charge you amounts greater than the sum of the parts to walk out of our shops with your lunch.

You will realise, however, that quality and consistency are the hardest things to achieve with repeated success, day in and day out. Over the years we have refined

and simplified in order to know that we can provide both. Our combinations are really considered with a thoroughness that is sometimes laughable (6 g of pine nuts or 7 g? 4 slices of cucumber or 5?) but it does matter (to us anyway) that we get it right (in our subjective opinion, it's true). Of course there are occasions when something goes awry — and we'd always like to know when a customer is disappointed by anything we do — but we hope that our formulae will go some way to ensuring satisfaction and deliciousness time and time again.

Your interpretation of this book and the way you use it (or not) is the next stage in the development of a theme and ideas surrounding that theme. If the words (recipes) inspire you to play around in the kitchen, experimenting and inventing, then we shall be delighted. If you use the book to recreate precisely the things we sell, we shall be flattered — as long as it is not on a commercial basis! Overall, we'd like to think that the fun we have in our kitchens can be enjoyed by you too.

WHAT CAN YOU DO?

When you make things at home you can go wild with shapes and sizes, you can improvise in any way you choose — or stick closely to our recipes if you prefer.

Sandwiches and salads are often made on a whim, after a fridge-raid or store-cupboard trawl. The better and broader the range of supplies, the more exciting the end result and so it is worth having some jolly good leftovers lurking about.

COMBINATIONS THAT WORK WELL

Many of our traditional British combinations have been served for generations as 'meat and two veg'. In Britain we use our best ingredients in great partnerships with accompaniments that bring out the flavours particularly well. The flavours tend to be quite pronounced — either hot or pungent like mustard and horseradish; vinegary or acidic like pickled cucumbers or capers; or sweet and sour like chutney and mint or cranberry sauces. All of these traditional combinations can be adapted for putting into sandwiches so that you might end up with the whole of Sunday (or Christmas) lunch clamped between two slices of bread. Sometimes the presentation needs refinement or the attention to quality a little more determined, but little else needs to change.

The remarkable craving for ever more exotic or unusual eating experiences means that we now have huge variety (much of it fun and adventurous). That is good. As long as we don't forget the best from the past, new additions are welcome.

Following is a list of some of the most well-known examples. Try them, then go on to invent your own. There are no rules and nothing should be branded as 'wrong'; so much is a matter of taste — personal taste, of course (eating is *all* about taste) — and preferences are schooled by experience, expectation and individual appetite.

Always try to use the best ingredients. Not expensive ingredients. Just the best quality available, as long as it is affordable. If it isn't, use something else that's a reasonable price; inexpensive but not a bargain — 'bargain' foods are likely to be cheaper for a reason. Possibly, in the case of meat, it may be because it has been pumped with water and salts that absorb water — so you will basically be paying for water when what you had hoped for was meat. Surprisingly (or maybe not) if you are eating really top-quality meat, you actually need/want to eat less of it.

THE OLD FAVOURITES

★ Beef and horseradish

★ Turkey and cranberry

★ Pork and apple

★ Ham and English mustard or piccalilli

★ Cod and tartare sauce

★ Skate and black butter

★ Sausage and marmalade

★ Duck and orange

★ Chicken and bread sauce

★ Smoked salmon and lemon

★ Pickled herring and sour cream

SANDWICH-FILLING SELECTION

Choosing sandwich fillings is like choosing what to wear — so many possibilities, many of them great, but sadly only one outfit is needed at a time. The weather, temperature and time of day are all relevant. And then there is the issue of taste. Not everyone wants to combine clashing colours or multiple layers; some prefer simplicity and understatement to racy risk-taking. (Risk-taking in sandwich making? Whatever next.)

Taking two slices of bread and making the decision of what to put between them is not exactly an intellectual exercise but it can be surprisingly challenging — there's really too much choice.

At Pret we spend hours pondering the issue. Picking winners is not a scientific process — but twenty years of practice helps give us an inkling of the things that really don't work or that work really well if eaten immediately but not after a few hours of hanging around. We try so many permutations and combinations, not only of ingredients but, equally important, how they are positioned within the sandwich. Is it better to put the crunch at the top (or bottom, if you are standing on your head) or in the middle? Should the seasoning be sprinkled over the protein or the leaves? Mayonnaise or butter, neither or both? Even the angle of cutting and the thickness of slicing make a difference to the final experience of taste and texture within a sandwich.

Our decisions are based on the possibilities from a limited range of ingredients. We deliberately restrict our range because we can monitor quality far more effectively with fewer supplies — and that matters to us (a lot). At home, of course, there are no restrictions and you can experiment with variety and eccentricity.

At Pret, we not only try to dream up the best (most exciting/most satisfying/most practical) combinations, but we are also rather keen to make sure that the ingredients will last intact — without browning, drying or going soggy — before they are eaten. Again, this is something that will be less of a problem at home but it is worth bearing in mind a few scientific principles — some are pretty obvious really, others not:

★ Ingredients should be of the same temperature (more or less): add cold to cold and hot to hot. For example, if making a ham and scrambled egg sandwich, both ingredients should ideally be at room temperature or both chilled. Don't add hot scrambled egg to cold ham unless you are going to eat it immediately. The heat from the egg will provide the most delightful breeding temperature for any bacteria lurking on or near the ham.

★ Think about the temperature of bacon when just cooked if you're about to add a dollop of mayonnaise; too hot and the mayo will melt to an oily puddle — which would still be delicious but not the intention — so put something in between like a slice of tomato or, even better, a piece of cheese which will enjoy melting.

★ Bread soaks up liquid as keenly as a sponge. Decide whether or not you want it to adopt this role and, if not, keep them apart. Lemon juice, vinegar and oil, for example, can be added to the filling ingredients rather than the sandwich base.

★ Butter can protect the bread from becoming soggy for quite a long time and it also stops the bread from seeming dry. And, if you are leaving bread that is already sliced exposed to the air, either wrap in cling film or, to be more environmentally friendly, cover with a clean, damp tea towel to stop it from becoming stale.

★ Mayonnaise — which we use far more than butter (and some people get quite miffed about it) — is an excellent coating; it spreads easily, the consistency can be varied, it can be flavoured with all sorts of exciting things, it keeps well and it tastes great with (almost) anything. While there are some very good mayonnaises to buy, there's also an easy way to make your own (see Basics chapter, page 236).

★ We tend to restrict our fillings to one type of protein at a time — no reason, more habit — but it would be fun to try surf 'n' turf in a sandwich.

★ Consider the three most important aspects of any food combination: flavour, texture and appearance. Balance salty foods with something less seasoned and creamy ones with a spot of acidity. Have a combination of crunchy and smooth ingredients. Colour in a sandwich is not essential — most of the filling is hidden — but it does make a difference if you are trying to tempt others to try your inventions. If it looks lively (not riotously so, but some green or red in an otherwise all-brown sandwich) it also looks more enticing.

FRIDGE RAIDS

Having said all of the above, one of the most satisfying and delicious ways of making a sandwich is to raid the fridge and combine whatever you find, within reason (perhaps it's best to leave out the nail varnish — yes, nail varnish is best kept refrigerated). Those leftovers may not look beautiful, semi-congealed on a plate or scrunched up in cling film, but once you've slapped them between two slices of gloriously fresh bloomer or rye or malted grain or a yawning length of baguette you won't see the imperfections, you will only be aware of the miraculous way in which flavours have matured and mingled like no spanking new, freshly assembled filling can begin to emulate. Some of your creations will be so successful that you will start to make 'leftovers' from scratch and on purpose. Often the combinations are perfect and yet, try as you might, you simply can't remember how you got there. Make notes if you find this happening too often.

Here are some notes on fridge finds or lurking leftovers:

★ Shepherd's pie? Add some sliced caperberries (not capers, which are buds, but the berries from the same plant which are milder and juicier) and perhaps a spot of diced tomato to freshen the texture.

★ A few desultory roasted veg? Mix with humous and finely chopped spring onions (scallions) on toasted ciabatta.

★ Lamb daube/casserole/stew? Do remove the cold, congealed fat. Lamb fat when not sizzling hot is an experience to be avoided. The meat itself will be delicious and can be combined with redcurrant jelly and some watercress salad on a chunky wholemeal (whole-wheat) loaf.

★ Smoked salmon trimmings? Yes, unlikely to find many of them hanging about, but you never know. Take out the mustard (any sort), add a small pinch of sugar, a teaspoon each of vinegar and crème fraîche or yoghurt or cream and some chopped dill (fresh or dry). A brown bread or rye would be ideal for this (or some blinis?) and it can be left open — perfectly attractive.

★ Chicken casserole, beef stew? Perfect. Add a dollop of mayonnaise, that's all. Use the meat and the carrots, onions, mushrooms and some of the fantastic jellied stock too. The stock should remain jellied but it will lose some of its solidity if it warms up too much, so just make sure that the bread is in thick doorsteps to mop it up.

★ Salad. Yes. The tired, flaccid remains of a once-crisp salad are one of the treats of a fridge-raider's dreams. The dressing has been thoroughly absorbed by all the ingredients — the bits of brown avocado, the hardboiled egg slices, the limp lettuce, artichoke hearts, capers, anchovies — and they taste glorious. All that is needed is some wonderful crisp-crusted white bread. In fact, hollow out a crisp white roll, tear the inside doughy bit to pieces and mix them in with the salad then place the whole lot back into the roll casing, squeeze it together and bite into it. This has a fancy name when it is started as a specific recipe — *pan bagnat*.

★ Bits of grilled or poached fish. Mix with mayo, finely chopped capers, gherkins (pickles) and dill weed to pile between slices of rye or in a white roll.

★ Soufflé remains? Hard to imagine that there would ever be any left-over soufflé — it always seems to disappear far too fast. But, should you find yourself in the lucky position of staring at a lump of solid soufflé, whether it is cheese, spinach or even chocolate, it will taste absolutely delicious (if it did when hot) in a sandwich. Try adding a spot of chutney or mustard to anything savoury and some crème fraîche or cream and a few raspberries or slices of mango to the chocolate version, then slapping it between slices of malted grain bread — life doesn't get much better. It's something to do with the texture (as usual) and also the fact that the flavours have had time to mingle and mature into a subtly sophisticated state. Rather pretentious to refer to cold food in this way, but these really are experiences to envy.

Many leftovers can be tarted up with finely sliced spring onions (scallions). The green parts are less aggressive than the white bulb ends and look good too. Don't always slice them into rings, try long elegant strips — the finer they are the better.

PRET PRODUCTS AS INGREDIENTS

We would be delighted (flattered) if you felt that some of our things could be adapted (improved upon?) to your own tastes with a spot of tweaking and alteration. We even have some suggestions:

★ Nuts. Use them in salads, on muesli, as a topping for pies and crumbles.

★ Crimble Crumble. Crumble up to use on your own crumble.

★ Berries. Add to muesli; poach them in syrup; marinate them in gin; chop them to make a sort of mincemeat (or a variation on the theme of mincemeat); cook them with roast duck, pork or venison; use in stuffings; serve them with cheese.

★ Juices. Add alcohol and retire to a shady bower; pour over fruit salads; use as a base for a marinade; add to pie fillings instead of sugar and water.

★ Crisps. Crunch over salads; use for dips; crush and use with herbs, beaten egg, breadcrumbs and butter in a crust for chops; serve with game.

★ Popcorn. Take to the cinema.

★ Soups. Use as a base for a casserole or marinade.

★ Pots. Serve with cake as a pudding; use as a pavlova topping with fresh fruits added; mix with oats and fruits and leave overnight for muesli in the morning.

★ Cakes. Soak with sherry and use as a base for trifle; cut into small squares and dust with sugar to use as petits fours; cut into small squares and dip in chocolate, again for petits fours; serve with fruit salad and cream; whizz in food processor with double (thick/heavy) cream and freeze as ice cream.

A JOKE

Three builders mixing cement on the 32nd floor of a building stop for their lunch break. They sit on a ledge and take out their lunch boxes.

The first one looks into his and sobs, 'Not beef *again*! I can't stand it.' The second man peers into his lunch box and lets out a wail, 'Oh no, it's mutton pie *again*, I can't stand it.' The third fellow opens his and bursts into tears, 'Soda bread and cheese *again*, I can't stand it.'

They all agree that life is simply not worth living and after scribbling notes to their wives they jump off the building, killing themselves. At the lavish funeral, funded by a stunned foreman and building company, the three wives try to console each other. They have each read their husband's note.

The first man's wife says, 'He need only have asked for something different.' The second man's wife says, 'If only I'd known, I'd have given him something different.' The third man's wife says, 'I just don't understand … he always made his own sandwiches.'

7.30AM

THE MORNING RUSH

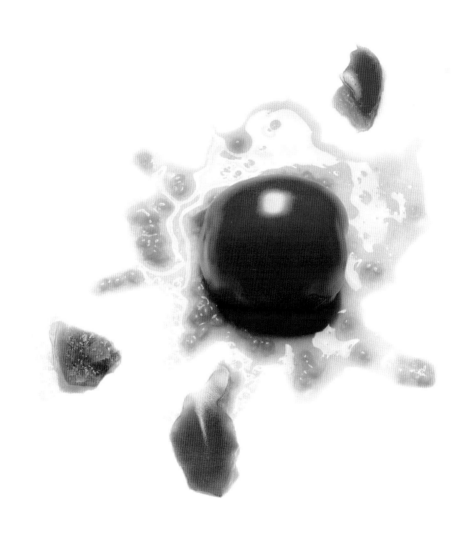

IN THE THERMOS

Instead of lugging a plastic bottle of lukewarm spring(-ish) water wherever you go, swap it for a natty thermos flask stuffed with ice cubes. The ice will slowly return to its watery, thirst-quenching state and you can coolly (no pun intended) offer it around to an appreciative — but possibly previously teasing — audience. Or try some of our other ideas …

★ IN THE THERMOS ★ IN THE THERMOS ★ IN THE THERMO

N THE THERMOS ★ IN THE THERMOS ★ IN THE THERMOS ★

What is it about thermos flasks? There is something intrinsically cosy and comforting about them. They were once only considered for lugging about rather hideously sweet, milky tea or instant coffee on long car journeys, at a time when motorway service stations were even less appealing than they are now. There was always the *frisson* of fear that the inner-glass vacuum capsule would shatter and that the white, plastic, flimsy-handled cup would receive shards of glass along with whatever hot liquid had been secured in the flask before setting off, full of anticipation, many hours before.

There is a new generation of flask. The sound and sensible metal-lined innovation, which seems to have been welcomed with not a murmur of disapproval. So the thermos is still alive, well and full of the promise of comfort, to be dispensed steamily into waiting mugs.

But why does one tend to concentrate on the preservation of heat — for icy, windswept hikes — when cold temperatures, for steamy days, can be as effectively maintained? Why not fill the flask with frothy milkshakes (the froth will subside but the concept and flavour remain charmingly intact) or ice cream floats? (Though not at the same time; apparently a well-known English football player attended a training session extolling the qualities of the thermos flask — hot things would remain hot and cold ones cold. When asked by the team manager what he had put in the flask he was cradling fondly, his proud response was 'a cup of tea and a choc ice'!) Ice-cold soups and smoothies to be sipped by the sea, or cocktails at the races need only the last-minute addition of a mint leaf or cucumber slice to lend suave sophistication to so worthy a piece of kit.

A few notes of obvious advice: heat the flask really well, in advance of adding hot foods or drinks, by filling it first with some lukewarm water and then, when after a few minutes it has become acclimatised to the warmth, replacing this with a hotter brew (this highlights another advantage of the glass liner's demise as it was pretty likely to crack if too hot a liquid caught it unawares). Alternatively, chill it in the freezer or fill it with ice cubes for at least 15 minutes before using it as a cooler. Best to remove the ice before adding the drink — it takes up too much space and will obviously dilute the contents when melted. You could always allocate one thermos specifically to store ice cubes for adding to drinks as they are poured.

If you're keen to have coffee or tea — decent, drinkable, life-enhancing tea and coffee — it is strongly recommended that the thermos be used for the transporting of the hot water 'neat' and that all the blending and brewing be carried out at whichever remote location has been picked. Neither of these hot drinks benefits one jot from being carted about ready-made. There is absolutely nothing to stop you from taking a cafetiere or plunger of ground coffee (all measured out) or a jug and strainer, or whichever preferred brewing equipment is selected, and adding the water from the comfort of deckchair, picnic rug or boot of the car. This will certainly work best with coffee because the temperature of the water can be (and should be) well below boiling: herbal teas will also be fine, while for black tea brewing, results will never be above okay-ish because 100°C (212°F) will have disappeared hours earlier.

DRINKS

Coffee and chocolate

One of Pret's particular passions is coffee. We pride ourselves on having thought really hard about the coffee we serve and not simply about flavour, but also the ethical issues. Ian Watson, our Head of Food, knows (almost) all there is to know on the subject of bean culture (although he's terribly modest about it) and he is constantly reviewing policy and developing ideas — the latest of which is an unbelievably exciting machine that gives us melted dark chocolate on tap, to mix with shots of espresso for the ultimate kick or, alternatively, in a more gentle combination with cappuccino froth.

We train some Team Members to be Baristas, recognisable by their black outfits (but not to be confused with the legal variety in black gowns and wigs) who learn all about beans and machines, water pressure and milk frothing, not to mention the 'crema' (the froth on top of an espresso that tells an expert exactly how good their technique really is).

There is very little of our coffee expertise that we can pass on for you to DIY — largely because much of it is linked rather specifically to the expensive machinery that we install in our shops (roughly equal to the cost of a small car — so if you don't mind taking the bus, you could have one installed at home and we'll tell you how to use it).

So, what can we advise you to do, armed with your thermos flask and raring to go? Well, much as we'd love to sell you many cups of coffee, don't come to ask us to fill the flask — within a very short time the coffee would be unrecognisable as a civilised drink. We'd rather you trained your taste buds with our beans and then went off in search of your own. Once found, grind them (or have them ground for you) and put them in an airtight bag or little tin, then take them with you together with a thermos of hot water (certainly doesn't want to be boiling for coffee making), a jug and a tea strainer, or a plunger coffee pot if that is the method of brewing you prefer. If using a jug — and to

⟣ PASSION FACT ⟢

Just Roasted. Like bread, coffee beans go stale. Big coffee companies
keep schtum about this. The truth is, after a couple of weeks the
flavour goes out the window. Anyway, we get 'Just Roasted' beans
delivered every day to every Pret. Coffee beans not used quickly
go to the compost heap. We grind a generous 14 grams of 'Just
Roasted' into every Pret cup. Our Barista Council is obsessive.
Our milk is organic and has been for yonks.

be completely honest, it produces some of the best coffee ever — your only problem will be what to do with the dregs, but it's not insurmountable. A jug is so simple and doesn't have the romantic allure of complex paraphernalia, but it works and all you have to do is put the coffee grounds in the bottom of the jug, pour on the water and wait (don't even stir anything). After a full five minutes, during which time the coffee will brew and many of the grounds will sink to the bottom of the jug, you should take your tea strainer, suspend it over a cup and dispense your brew.

Where chocolate is concerned, the thermos is pretty perfect. Melt the chocolate in a bain-marie (or a bowl over a pan of simmering water) and decant it into the warmed flask. When basking in some remote spot with a delicate feast spread before you, reach into a bag to retrieve some meringues or profiteroles, unscrew the thermos lid and nonchalantly pour melted chocolate over everything (well, not quite) pausing only to ask your guests whether they would prefer their pudding with or without the cream that you have thoughtfully stowed in another flask.

Tea

Making a nice cuppa for a thermos is not a particularly good idea. The main problem is one of temperature because black tea (which is what we drink) needs boiling water and, however boiling the water might have been in the kettle, it loses heat wildly fast and by the time the thermos cap is unscrewed the contents would produce something barely palatable.

So, for 'tea' time, carry along some iced tea — made with Earl Grey or Lapsang Souchong, a hint of sugar, some lemon juice and lots of mint. Or, take some fresh mint and the thermos filled with as much hot water as possible and a pretty teapot to brew on arrival at your chosen drinking spot.

Pineapple and mango yoghurt drink
Serves 2

INGREDIENTS | 2 mangoes, roughly chopped
$\frac{1}{2}$ pineapple, roughly chopped
100 ml ($3\frac{1}{2}$ fl oz) fresh apple juice
500 g (1 lb 2 oz) bio yoghurt
1 lime, juice and zest

PUT THE MANGO and pineapple into a blender or food processor with the apple juice and whizz until smooth. Add the yoghurt and blend further.

Add the lime juice and zest and stir through (rather than blend) just a little — this keeps the lime flavour sharp and concentrated. Drink immediately or, if left for a while, add some more lime juice because the first lot will tend to have been absorbed.

If you enjoy very cold drinks, keep the fruits — except bananas, which go black — in the fridge until you are about to use them. Alternatively, you could add some ice, bearing in mind that this will weaken the intensity of the flavour and the texture too. Another possibility would be to whizz the mango to a purée in advance and then freeze as ice cubes. Makes a lot of noise in the blender (which can be hard to bear early in the morning), but the end result is good — and cold.

Elderflower Pure Pret Still
Makes 500 ml (17 fl oz) cordial

INGREDIENTS | 300 g (10½ oz) caster (superfine) sugar
500 ml (17 fl oz) boiling water
1 large whole lemon (see Note), chopped or whizzed in food processor
10 elderflower heads, shaken well to remove insects

DISSOLVE THE SUGAR in the water in a large bowl. Add the lemon and flowers. Cover the bowl with cling film and leave for 24 hours in a cool place.

Strain the liquid through a muslin cloth (or thin tea towel) and pour into a sterilised bottle. This can be stored in the fridge for up to 3 months. Splash some of the elderflower cordial into a glass and add sparkling or still mineral water to taste.

NOTE If the lemon appears to have a large number of pips, it would be a good idea to remove as many as possible before blending to avoid the bitterness that they sometimes impart.

Elderflowers lurk prettily in the hedgerows of Britain in early summer. The delicacy of their appearance in no way prepares one for the intensity of flavour that they hold. It is remarkably easy to capture that flavour in a syrup to store it for use in all sorts of things; whack it into cream instead of vanilla essence to serve with a pudding; add it to fruit salad; put it on your morning muesli with some yoghurt — all quite apart from simply drinking it as a Pure Pret Still.

Vitamin volcanoes

If you gather enough freshly squeezed or puréed fruit and vegetable juice you will be unable to avoid vitamin overload — the feeling that you could quite easily conquer the world before breakfast and then fight on some more. Hence 'volcanoes'.

Try to make the drinks just before consuming them — the vitamins do lose their power if kept hanging around, which is the only reason to suggest that you make these at home rather than popping into a Pret. Our smoothies and juices are as fresh as can be and stuffed to the gunwales with vitamins, but there is no substitute for just-made.

The following make good combinations and take no time at all in a food processor. If you consider having two or three pieces of fruit or veg in each drink, you will be able to work out quantities to suit you. Adding yoghurt, milk or coconut milk will, inevitably, make them even more filling but don't be fooled into thinking that because these drinks are healthy they are low in calories — they're not. You may need to consider them as an entire meal — a new take on a liquid lunch.

If you feel like adding ice, bear in mind how diluting the melted cubes will be and season everything well to counter the effect. Sweeten with honey or dark brown sugar if and where necessary. Sharpen with lemon or lime juice but, in some cases, adding yoghurt will have the same result.

With all the suggestions to follow, the juiciness of the fruit or vegetables will vary and you may well need to add water to dilute things. You can choose whether to use still water or one with a slight fizz.

You may feel that your attempts at smoothies don't approach the velvety luxury of shop ones. Bear in mind that often the bulk of a smoothie is either banana — which is a very effective filler (and nothing wrong with that) — or it may be apple juice or grape juice, both of which are sweet and have suitable temperaments for all-round adaptability. You may prefer to use juices to dilute the mixture in preference to water.

The addition of spices — like cinnamon, ginger or nutmeg — can pose a presentation problem if the flecks of ground spice hover on the surface, rather than blending effectively with the juice. If that is the case, you could make a sugar syrup, flavouring it with whichever spice you fancy, as the boiling together with sugar and water will help accommodate the ground powder. Don't worry too much about quantities and proportions — what you are after is a carrier and as long as the end result is not too watery (which would mean too much additional liquid in the smoothie) you'll be fine. For savoury concoctions, the flecks of spice somehow don't seem as intrusive.

VOLCANOES

Apple, orange and banana (old favourite)

Apple, cinnamon, honey and a dash of crème fraîche

Avocado, strawberry and orange with mint

Avocado, watercress and yoghurt with fennel seeds

Raw beetroot and yoghurt with lemon

Celery and cucumber with dill and black pepper

Raspberry and blueberry with a spoonful of yoghurt

Mango and avocado with lime

Carrot and ginger

Spinach and yoghurt with nutmeg

Cranberry, ginger and apple

Pomegranate and raspberry

Tomato, yoghurt and coriander (cilantro)

Grapefruit, lime and mint

Papaya, lime, orange and coconut

SOUPS

Soups, like sandwiches, can be made from almost anything. The combining of ingredients is straightforward: meat or fish, vegetables and liquid and that's it (well, almost). They can be cooked or raw, smooth or chunky. Our most successful soups — created by the great Soup Man, Nick Sandler (who also happens to be our Creative Chef) — are the 'main course' soups like Spaghetti Bolognaise Soup and Chilli Beef Soup. So, if you're feeling inventive and daring, make your favourite supper dish and dilute it with some stock and a dash of cream or crème fraîche and you will have a stunning, original soup. In the summer you can use the same recipes as for winter soups, but serve them cold (though, this works best with smooth, rather than chunky, concoctions).

It's quite important, when considering the make-or-break minutiae of the soup world, to mention stocks. There is no doubt (absolutely none) that if you have a stunning proper stock to provide the foundation, you really cannot go wrong. Even if you were inadvertently to add too much salt, all could be put right with the addition of water, as the intrinsic quality would still be there. This is the sort of intangible 'body' that a stock cube or powder simply can't provide. So, with this in mind, what are we going to do to help you on your way?

Well, here is a crash course on how to make chicken stock (or any poultry or game stock), which is not only dead easy but arguably the most versatile to have lurking about. You can even become so attached to it that you won't even progress to the other recipes in the book. So, off we go: Gather as many chicken or turkey or game bones and skin, cooked or raw, as you can. Put them in a large saucepan and cover them with cold water. If you have them, add any or all of the following, not in great quantity but a stick, or a slice or two of: onion (and the brown crinkly skin is good too because it gives the stock a good colour), carrot, celery and parsley stalks (but not the leaves because they have relatively little flavour and they can compromise the colour of the stock).

Don't add: chicken liver, because it goes bitter, or turnips or parsnips, or even garlic, because their flavours are far too intrusive, or salt, because you will be wanting to reduce the stock by boiling (to get the velvety, gelatinous texture that real stock is all about) and that will concentrate flavour (seasoning) and therefore saltiness, dramatically.

Bring the whole lot to the boil (a lid on the pan will speed things up) and then turn down the heat so that everything simmers in a gentle way. If the stock boils at a rapid pace it will be less clear (in fact it will be cloudy) because the particles of fat that inevitably escape from the skin and bones emulsify in the water. Cloudy stock is not a disaster by any means, only less beautiful — if conducted at a graceful simmer, the fat stays on its own and can be skimmed off with ease later on.

The simmering stage can be continued for hours. The pan could even be put in a low oven (100°C/200°F/Gas 1/2) and left overnight. Minimum time for the bones and water to be in close proximity would be about 2 hours — although it is possible to create an adequate chicken-flavoured infusion in about 20 minutes (but that is not what we are talking about here). Strain the stock from the bones and throw the bones (and all the other odds and ends) away. Apart from skimming the fat off the surface you are ready with a pretty exciting product.

If you are using the stock straightaway, then on you go with soup making. If you would like to keep it (or some of it) to use later, then rather than having large quantities of liquid sloshing about in your fridge, you can boil it right down and fill ice cube trays for freezing or, and this is where it becomes really exciting, you may find that having boiled it down, the consistency is so jellied and thick that you can store it (again in ice cube portions) in the fridge as real, live stock cubes, ready to be whipped out at a moment's notice and taken on a jaunt with the thermos full of hot water and the thrill of your own instant cup of soup! (Take along a few chopped spring onions (scallions), some single (whipping) cream and maybe a dash of sherry or Tabasco for ultimate excitement.) You would need to season the stock before the reduction to get it to the exact flavour that you would want and then boil away. It will become alarmingly concentrated but when you reconstitute it, the flavour will be perfect.

Stock — strained, clear stock — should last happily in a fridge for a week. If vegetables are still bathing in it, however, they will 'turn' the stock (even in the cold) after only a few days, so it is important to be strict about hauling them out. It is possible to extend the keeping time almost indefinitely by taking the stock out of the fridge daily and boiling it for a good five minutes (a rollicking, spluttering boil) and then cooling it as quickly as possible by standing the pan in a sink filled with ice-cold water, and then popping it back into the fridge again.

Roasted root vegetable soup
Serves 4

INGREDIENTS

2 parsnips, roughly diced

½ celeriac, roughly diced

3 carrots, roughly diced

¼ swede (rutabaga), roughly diced

2 tbsp olive oil

1 onion, roughly diced

2 sticks celery, chopped

30 g (1 oz) butter

1 litre (35 fl oz) vegetable stock (Marigold is our favourite)

2 waxy potatoes, roughly diced

a few rosemary sprigs, fresh or dried

some sage, fresh or dried

2 bay leaves

sea salt and coarse-ground black pepper

a splash of white wine vinegar or balsamic would be delicious

ROAST THE FIRST FOUR root vegetables, coated with the olive oil and a sprinkling of salt, in a hot oven (220°C/425°F/Gas 7) for about 20 minutes.

In a large saucepan, gently fry the onion and celery in the butter until soft. Add the stock, potato, rosemary, sage and bay leaves and bring to the boil. Simmer until the potato is soft, about 20 minutes.

Remove only the bay leaves and blend all remaining saucepan ingredients until smooth. Return to the saucepan,

add the roasted vegetables and reheat, stirring to prevent it catching on the bottom. Season with salt and pepper if necessary and, if it needs a little sharpening, add a splash of white wine vinegar or balsamic vinegar.

NOTE This soup has been described as a vegetarian roast dinner in a bowl. The veg are roasted with olive oil and then drowned in a warming winter broth. We can't think of a more glamorous way to go (for a root vegetable).

Field and forest mushroom soup
Serves 4

INGREDIENTS

30 g (1 oz) unsalted butter

1 tsp garlic purée (or 1 clove garlic, finely chopped)

1 onion, diced

1 waxy potato, diced

1 stick celery, diced

2 carrots, diced

100 g (3½ oz) mixed mushrooms, cleaned well

1 litre (35 fl oz) chicken stock (see recipe on page 42) or water

salt and coarse-ground black pepper

a splash of white wine vinegar (optional)

100 ml (3½ fl oz) single (whipping) cream

2 tbsp finely chopped flat-leaf parsley

MELT THE BUTTER in a large heavy-based saucepan. Add the garlic and onion and cook over low heat for 3 minutes, so that the onion softens rather than becomes crisp and fried. Throw in the rest of the vegetables, stir and continue cooking for a further 3–5 minutes. Add the stock, stir, cover the saucepan with a lid and turn up the heat. Let the stock come to a boil, turn down the heat slightly and simmer everything until the vegetables are soft.

Just before serving, adjust the seasoning — if the whole thing needs sparking up a little, add a splash of vinegar — and then add the cream and parsley. Do not allow to boil at this point or the cream could curdle. Serve with crunchy, garlicky bread.

Malaysian chicken soup
Serves 4

CURRY PASTE	½ tsp dried red chilli flakes, reconstituted in boiling water
	2 cloves garlic, finely chopped
	3 cm (1¼ in) length galangal, thickest piece possible, finely chopped
	1½ tsp ground turmeric
	2 red chillies, seeded and finely chopped
	1 stick lemon grass, finely chopped
	2 red Asian shallots, finely chopped
	1 tbsp vegetable oil
SOUP	1 litre (35 fl oz) chicken stock (see recipe on page 42)
	2 floury potatoes, roughly diced
	1 large sweet potato, roughly diced
	200 ml (7 fl oz) coconut cream
	2 large, skinless, boneless chicken thighs, cut into chunks
	2 tbsp fish sauce (nam pla)
	3 spring onions (scallions), sliced
	1 lime, freshly squeezed

TO MAKE THE RENDANG curry paste, gently fry all the paste ingredients together for about 20 minutes, stirring occasionally. Whizz everything in the food processor or blender until smooth — you may need to add a little water to help the process. Sieve or strain to remove the more aggressive fibres of lemon grass and galangal.

Add the stock to the curry paste in a large saucepan. Add the potatoes, bring to the boil and simmer for about 20 minutes. Blend everything in a food processor when the potatoes are soft. Return to the saucepan. Add the sweet potato, coconut cream and chicken pieces and cook for about 10 minutes, or until the sweet potato is soft and the chicken cooked through. Add the fish sauce, spring onion and lime juice and serve.

Celeriac and parsley mash soup
Serves 4

INGREDIENTS

2 carrots, chopped

1 onion, chopped

30 g (1 oz) unsalted butter

1 large celeriac, chopped

1 litre (35 fl oz) vegetable stock (Marigold is our favourite)

2 bay leaves

rosemary leaves, fresh or dried

sage leaves, fresh or dried

sea salt and coarse-ground black pepper

ground nutmeg

100 ml (3½ fl oz) double (thick/heavy) cream

generous handful of roughly chopped flat-leaf parsley

IN A SAUCEPAN, gently soften the carrots and onion in the butter over medium heat. Add the celeriac, vegetable stock, bay leaves, rosemary and sage, increase the heat and bring to the boil. Then reduce the heat and allow to simmer for 25 minutes, or until all the vegetables are soft.

Remove the bay leaves and blend the soup in a food processor or with a hand blender roughly or until smooth (your choice). Season with salt, pepper and nutmeg. Stir through the cream and parsley and serve with the freshest, crunchiest bread you can find.

This simple and delicious soup is based on seasonal winter vegetables. It's thick and stuffed full of creamy celeriac.

Five bean cassoulet soup

Serves 4

INGREDIENTS

1 onion, diced

1 clove garlic, finely chopped

1 red chilli, finely chopped

3 carrots, diced

2 sticks celery, diced

1 tbsp olive oil

2 floury potatoes, roughly diced

1 litre (35 fl oz) vegetable stock (Marigold is our favourite)

200 g (7 oz) each of cooked butterbeans (lima beans), borlotti (cranberry) beans, cannellini beans, red kidney beans, flageolet beans (see Note)

1 tbsp sun-dried tomato paste (concentrated purée)

1 tsp mild paprika

1 tbsp balsamic vinegar

rosemary leaves, fresh or dried

sage leaves, fresh or dried

TO SERVE

flat-leaf parsley, roughly chopped

real mayo (Basics, page 236) mixed with as much crushed garlic as you dare

FRY THE FIRST FIVE ingredients in the oil in a large saucepan for 5 minutes. Add the potato and stock and simmer for 10–15 minutes, or until the potato is soft. Blend everything until smooth and return to the pan.

Add all the remaining ingredients, except the parsley and mayonnaise, and simmer for a further 10 minutes, stirring every now and then to check that nothing is sticking to the bottom of the pan. Serve in large bowls with the parsley scattered over and a spoonful of mayonnaise plonked inelegantly but triumphantly in the middle.

NOTE All the beans are available in tins, pre-cooked. If you can't find one type or another, substitute with more of whichever you prefer, or try any other type that might be lurking. This saves time and the worry of the poisonous aspects of some semi-cooked (or raw) pulses. However, if you find yourself having to cook the beans yourself, don't worry, just allow a few days extra for preparation and reward yourself with a holiday afterwards. Soak them first (better to tackle them in individual batches rather than lumping them all together) in cold water for at least 12 hours. Make sure you use large bowls — they increase by $2^1/_2$–3 times in size — and allow 30 g (1 oz) of dried bean to yield 100 g ($3^1/_2$ oz) of final reconstituted bean. Cook them (also in separate batches, because they cook at different rates — just to be even more awkward) by boiling in water until they are really, really soft, which should take about 40 minutes (don't add salt, it toughens the skins). You could also bake them in the oven — again in water and covered with a lid — and this will also take about 40 minutes. As you can probably now see, tinned beans are rather tempting.

This is a vegetarian version of the Languedoc staple that is usually stuffed with Toulouse sausage and duck confit. By all means reinterpret the original and add all the meat you like to this recipe for a substantial and warming winter gut-buster. Otherwise, stay veggie and perhaps muster a seriously garlicky mayonnaise to add in heroic spoonfuls when serving.

✦ PASSION FACT ✦

Our freshly pressed carrot juice is part of our
range of 100% natural juices. It is packed full of vitamins
and nutrients and, unlike so many of today's trendy health
drinks, contains no chemicals or additives. Apparently
fresh carrot juice enjoys a bizarre reputation for helping to
fight the effects of jet lag ... Something to do with
antioxidants? Anyway, we sell it because it tastes good!

Arabian-spiced carrot soup
Serves 4

INGREDIENTS

450 g (1 lb) carrots, diced

1 onion, diced

2 cloves garlic, finely chopped

2 sticks celery, diced

1 tbsp olive oil

1 tsp ground cumin

1 tsp ground coriander

1/2 tsp ground turmeric

1 jalapeño chilli, chopped

1/2 tsp ground fenugreek

1 floury potato, diced

100 g (3 1/2 oz) tinned red lentils

1 tbsp sun-dried tomato paste (concentrated purée)

1 litre (35 fl oz) vegetable stock (Marigold is our favourite)

salt and coarse-ground black pepper

1 lemon, freshly squeezed

1/2 tsp nigella seeds

150 g (5 1/2 oz) labneh (Lebanese yoghurt)

1 large handful chopped flat-leaf parsley

FRY THE FIRST FOUR ingredients in the oil for about 5 minutes over medium–high heat. Add the spices and fry for a further minute, or until aromatic. Add the potato, lentils, tomato paste and stock and simmer for about 30 minutes, topping up with extra water if it is reducing too much.

Blend roughly, return to the saucepan and season with salt, pepper, lemon juice and the nigella seeds. Add the labneh and parsley and heat through, without allowing it to boil as it might curdle (which needn't be a disaster, it just means that the soup has little flecks of white and looks less smooth).

Prosciutto primavera soup
Serves 4

INGREDIENTS	
	30 g (1 oz) unsalted butter
	100 g (3½ oz) block of prosciutto, diced (see Note)
	1 onion, roughly chopped
	2 leeks, roughly chopped
	4 small new potatoes, unpeeled
	1 tsp chopped fresh thyme
	900 ml (31 fl oz) chicken stock (see recipe on page 42)
	200 g (7 oz) petits pois (peas)
	40 g (1½ oz) fresh white breadcrumbs
	100 g (3½ oz) crème fraîche
	Pret seasoning (Basics, page 251)
TO SERVE	3 spring onions (scallions), finely sliced
	a few sprigs of mint, roughly chopped

MELT THE BUTTER in a large saucepan, add the diced prosciutto, onion and leek and cook over a low heat for about 10 minutes. Add the potatoes, thyme and stock and simmer for 20–30 minutes, or until the potato is soft.

Stir in the peas and breadcrumbs and cook gently until everything begins to thicken. Add the crème fraîche, check the seasoning and serve with the spring onions and chopped mint.

NOTE If you cannot find a block of prosciutto, ask your delicatessen whether they can save you their next knuckle-end from a Parma ham or use pancetta, speck, Serrano or Bayonne ham instead.

Frozen *petits pois* (peas) are actually preferable to fresh. Strange as it may seem, they are sweeter and 'pop' rather delightfully when bitten. 'Fresh' ones tend to be older, more starchy and therefore more leaden.

Chicken, leek and potato soup
Serves 4

INGREDIENTS

2 leeks, with the green part still attached

1 onion, roughly chopped

2 sticks celery, roughly chopped

50 g (1¾ oz) unsalted butter

3 floury potatoes, roughly chopped

1 litre (35 fl oz) chicken stock (see recipe on page 42)

2 chicken thighs, skinless, boneless and cut into chunks

3 tbsp dry white wine

1 sprig of thyme

1 sprig of tarragon

3 bay leaves

100 ml (3½ fl oz) double (thick/heavy) cream

salt and coarse-ground black pepper

CUT THE GREEN LEAFY part of the leek from the white end. Roughly chop the green bits (make sure that any grit or soil has been washed away) and slice the white ends into rings. Fry the green leek pieces, onion and celery in the butter over low heat until softened, about 10 minutes. Add the potato and stock and bring to the boil. Then simmer until the potato is soft. Remove two large spoonfuls of the potato and keep to one side. Blend the remaining potato with the stock and other vegetables.

Return everything to the pan (except the reserved potato) and add the remaining leek, chicken, white wine and herbs. Simmer for 10 minutes, or until the leek and chicken are cooked. Put the reserved potato back into the soup and warm through. Add the cream and season with salt and pepper. Do not let it boil once the cream has been added.

VARIATIONS If you feel that the flavour of this soup needs brightening a little, add a squeeze of lemon juice or use yoghurt instead of cream, which has a more acidic flavour. (The no-boil rule still holds.) This soup could be served chilled in the summer. Add some chopped chervil for a splash of colour.

Chilli beef soup
Serves 4

INGREDIENTS

250 g (9 oz) minced (ground) beef

1 tbsp olive oil

1 onion, roughly diced

2 cloves garlic, finely chopped

1 red pepper (capsicum), roughly diced

1 small red chilli (medium strength), chopped

2 tsp ground cumin

2 tsp mild paprika

a pinch cayenne pepper

1 tbsp balsamic vinegar

750 ml (26 fl oz) chicken stock (see recipe on page 42)

3 tbsp tomato paste (concentrated purée)

3 bay leaves

400 g (14 oz) tinned chopped tomatoes

400 g (14 oz) kidney beans, cooked or from a tin

1 lime, freshly squeezed

salt

TO SERVE

soft tortillas

sour cream

FRY THE BEEF in the oil with the onion and garlic for a few minutes over medium–high heat. Add the pepper, chilli and spices and cook for 15 minutes. Add the vinegar, cook for a minute, then add the stock, tomato paste and bay leaves.

Blend the tomatoes with half the kidney beans until smooth. Add to the pan and simmer for 45 minutes, stirring every now and then to make sure that it doesn't catch at the bottom. If necessary, add some water to thin it down.

Finish with the remaining whole kidney beans and the lime juice. Check the seasoning, adding some salt if necessary. Serve with soft tortillas, and a dollop of sour cream in each bowl.

Christmas turkey and all the trimmings soup
Serves 4

INGREDIENTS

1 onion, roughly chopped

30 g (1 oz) unsalted butter

2 cloves garlic

2 tsp mild paprika

1 red pepper (capsicum), roughly chopped

100 g (3½ oz) bacon bits (lardons)

1 leek, roughly chopped

100 ml (3½ fl oz) red wine

1 litre (35 fl oz) turkey stock (made from the carcass of a Christmas turkey
— adapt recipe for chicken stock on page 42)

1 tbsp worcestershire sauce

4 tomatoes, roughly chopped

3 tbsp tomato paste (concentrated purée)

1 waxy potato (or 1 left-over roast potato), roughly chopped

1 sprig of thyme

3 bay leaves

cooked turkey, as much as possible

FRY THE ONION in the butter for a few minutes and then add the garlic, paprika, pepper, bacon and leek. Cook over medium heat for 15 minutes. Add the wine, increase the heat and boil until it has reduced by about half. Add the stock and all remaining ingredients except the turkey, reduce the heat and simmer for about 30 minutes so that the potato, if it started raw, is soft. If it was already cooked, the simmering will give all the ingredients time to mingle, which is no bad thing.

Add the turkey and check the seasoning. A dash of white wine vinegar might be a useful addition at this stage and, if there is some left-over stuffing or a few roasted chestnuts, throw them all in too.

Cream would elevate the overall appearance and sophistication, as would some finely chopped parsley or spring onions, but none of these is essential.

12.30PM

THE LUNCHTIME RUSH

THE LUNCH BOX

Pack a portable feast for work or an outing. Cram your favourite fresh, light and delicious Pret ideas into a cheeky little Chinese basket or a suave Japanese lunch box.

★ THE LUNCH BOX ★ THE LUNCH BOX ★ THE LUNCH BOX

THE LUNCH BOX ★ THE LUNCH BOX ★ THE LUNCH BOX ★

The Lunch Box is another comforting piece of equipment, associated with childhood and picnic outings. Packed lunches were a treat at school — though obviously not for the parent preparing it in the early hours of a cold, school morning — evoking for each child the essence of his or her home, from the moment the Tupperware lid was lifted and the smell of the kitchen wafted across the desk. The contents not only revealed the sandwich, meat pie, vegetable sticks or cake but also a slice of personal life from beyond the school gates.

Lunch boxes were also an insight into family favourites and the edible foibles or fancies of home. Sometimes the contents of the lunch box were a little too exotic — possibly the first time a fellow classmate might have clapped eyes on the candy-floss pink of taramasalata on half an avocado. This was sophistication in the early years of 'foodies'.

The contents of the lunch box are a distillation of the basics of a feast — or should be. A selection of tempting and, of course, healthy delicacies. They need to have been considered for transit and should not be so temperamental that they wilt whilst waiting to be consumed. These are two of the most important aspects we have to consider at Pret as we dream up the portable delights that you buy.

Another issue, and subject of much thought, is packaging. This has to be kept to a minimum — to reduce waste of materials — and also has to be simple in construction and deconstruction (how often have you had to fight your way into a bag?). Our packaging materials have to be safe and clean and attractive. In all honesty, we hate having to use ghastly packaging. In fact, we'd love to wrap our sandwiches in lettuce leaves (brilliant way to keep them fresh and stop them from drying out) but, well, it's just not practical. We'd love to fill red or yellow peppers (capsicums) with humous or guacamole (with carrot and celery sticks sticking out of the top) and let you crunch your way through them, rather than have to use plastic bowls, but again, impractical. So many possibilities, so little chance of us being able to use them — but you can.

What should the ideal lunch box hold? Luxury and hedonism aren't often associated with Tupperware or cling film, but there is no reason to be too prosaic about the contents. Even if the choice is a cheese sandwich and packet of crisps, make sure the sandwich sits proudly full of the best cheese and mouth-wateringly tempting pickle and the crisps have been made with top-quality vegetables (you can crisp anything these days), fried in wholesome oil and flavoured with natural seasonings — in fact, Pret crisps.

On the subject of hedonism, which brings to mind caviar, oysters and smoked halibut (washed down with a cheeky little white burgundy), these fellows don't actually benefit from travelling about in close confinement and you would be advised to use them in your home-based sandwich selection (please refer to Chapter 4). Best to stick to the stalwarts of sandwich society but to do so with style.

Pack yourself (or whomever it is you are treating) variety and nutritional balance — a bit of carbohydrate (unless you are consciously cutting carbs), some protein, lots of fresh, crisp salad or cold, roasted vegetables, something fruity maybe, and possibly (very possibly) a piece of chocolate. This chapter gives the recipes for the carb/protein/veg combinations, as well as salads and un-scary sushi. If you were thinking of avoiding breads (or rice, another carbohydrate) then simply use the fillings (or sushi toppings) alone or with a salad, increasing the quantities to compensate.

BAGUETTES

Egg and bacon

BAGUETTE	⅓ baguette
FILLING	65 g (2¼ oz) egg mayo (see recipe on page 82)
	Pret seasoning (Basics, page 251)
	2½ rashers cooked bacon

CUT THE BAGUETTE almost in half lengthways (leaving one edge still attached) and spread the mayonnaise over the bottom half; using two forks works best. Season, and place the bacon on top. Cover with the top half of the baguette, pressing down gently to keep everything in place.

We make these three breakfast baguettes for people to grab on the way to work in the mornings. They are shorter than our other baguettes but stuffed full of comforting, early morning sustenance — precisely the sort of thing you would knock together yourself, if only you didn't have to rush out.

Egg and roasted tomato

BAGUETTE | ⅓ baguette
FILLING | 65 g (2¼ oz) egg mayo (see recipe on page 82)
| Pret seasoning (Basics, page 251)
| 4 roasted tomato quarters

CUT THE BAGUETTE almost in half lengthways (leaving one edge still attached) and spread the mayonnaise over the bottom half. Season, and place the tomato quarters on top. Cover with the top half of the baguette, pressing down gently to keep everything in place.

Egg and smoked salmon

BAGUETTE | ⅓ baguette
FILLING | 65 g (2¼ oz) egg mayo (see recipe on page 82)
| Pret seasoning (Basics, page 251)
| 2 slices smoked salmon
| 1 handful mustard and cress

CUT THE BAGUETTE almost in half lengthways (leaving one edge still attached) and spread the mayonnaise over the bottom half. Season, and place the salmon on top. Sprinkle the mustard and cress haphazardly over the salmon. You could of course put mustard and cress (or rocket, or any sort of foliage) in the other baguettes too, but we don't. Cover with the top half of the baguette, pressing down gently to keep everything in place.

Chorizo baguette

BAGUETTE | ½ baguette
FILLING | 25 g (1 oz) real mayo (Basics, page 236)
| 3 slices grilled aubergine (eggplant)
| 4 slices mozzarella
| 5 slices chorizo

CUT THE BAGUETTE almost in half lengthways (leaving one edge still attached) and spread the mayonnaise over the bottom half. Evenly position the aubergine slices, followed by the mozzarella and finally the chorizo along the bread. Close with the top half of the baguette, pressing down gently to keep everything in place.

Classic tuna baguette

BAGUETTE | ½ baguette
FILLING | 80 g (2¾ oz) tuna mayo (Basics, page 241)
| 5 slices cucumber

SLICE THE BAGUETTE in half horizontally. Spread the tuna mayo over the bottom half. Arrange the slices of cucumber along the tuna in a neat row. Replace the top half of the baguette.

Venison baguette

BAGUETTE	½ baguette
FILLING	25 g (1 oz) real mayo (Basics, page 236)
	2 slices smoked or marinated venison
	Pret seasoning (Basics, page 251)
	5 slices tomato
	1 handful rocket (arugula) leaves

CUT THE BAGUETTE almost in half lengthways (leaving one edge still attached) and spread the mayonnaise over the bottom half. Arrange the venison slices over the mayo and season a little (the venison can sometimes be quite salty and may not need anything extra). Add the tomato slices and the rocket leaves as neatly as you feel appropriate (not much scope for wild behaviour here). Close with the top half of the baguette, pressing down gently to keep everything in place.

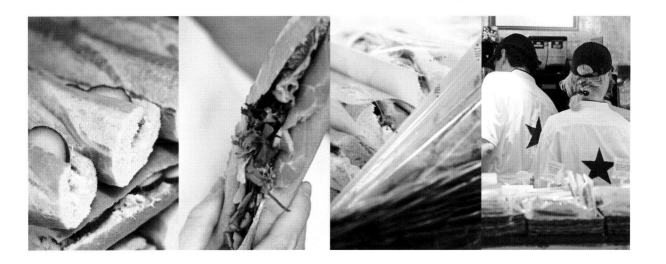

Super club baguette

BAGUETTE	½ baguette
FILLING	55 g (2 oz) cooked, roughly sliced or shredded chicken
	mixed with 25 g (1 oz) real mayo (Basics, page 236)
	Pret seasoning (Basics, page 251)
	2½ rashers cooked bacon
	4 slices tomato
	1 handful spinach leaves

CUT THE BAGUETTE almost in half lengthways (leaving one edge still attached) and spread the chicken and mayonnaise mix over the bottom half. Season, and arrange the bacon, tomato slices and spinach on top. Cover with the top half of the baguette, pressing down gently to keep everything in place.

★ THE LUNCH BOX ★ THE LUNCH BOX ★ THE LUNCH BOX

Char-grilled pepper baguette

BAGUETTE | ½ baguette
FILLING | 45 g (1½ oz) garlic and herb cream cheese (mix your own or use something like Boursin — see Notes)
| ½ char-grilled pepper (capsicum), grilled (broiled) if the barbecue happens to be out (see Notes)
| 1 handful rocket (arugula) leaves

CUT THE BAGUETTE almost in half lengthways (leaving one edge still attached) and spread the cream cheese over the bottom half. Arrange the peppers on top. Stuff the leaves in a heap into the far corners and all over the topping, so that each bite has some of the fresh peppery taste that rocket provides. Cover with the top half of the baguette, pressing down gently to keep everything in place.

NOTES Cream cheese is easily and effectively influenced by added flavours. It can be bought ready seasoned, but you can mix your own speciality with little effort.

Grilling peppers is also easy and you can use any colour (they all act the same way, the only difference being the level of sweetness, with red and yellow being far sweeter than green — because the green are less ripe versions of the others). They respond well by releasing their tough skins and then the flesh becomes wonderfully soft and succulent — completely in contrast to their raw crispness. Cut them in halves or quarters before grilling, brush them with a little olive oil (if you can't be bothered to brush, just dab with your fingers) and season with salt and pepper. The addition of a little anchovy essence or some garlic chunks can be rather successful as a flamboyant extra gesture.

THE LUNCH BOX ★ THE LUNCH BOX ★ THE LUNCH BOX ★

Ham, egg and Italian cheese baguette

BAGUETTE	½ baguette
FILLING	65 g (2¼ oz) egg mayo (see recipe on page 82)
	coarse-ground black pepper
	50 g (1¾ oz) dry-cured ham
	2–3 slices Italian matured cheese, such as parmesan or pecorino
	4 slices tomato
	1 handful spinach leaves

CUT THE BAGUETTE almost in half lengthways (leaving one edge still attached) and spread the mayonnaise over the bottom half; using two forks works best. Season with a few grinds of black pepper and arrange the ham, cheese and tomato on top. Cram in some leaves; their colour makes a great impact. Cover with the top half of the baguette, pressing down gently to keep everything in place.

⫷ PASSION FACT ⫸

Pret uses free-range eggs from farms
where there is no routine use of antibiotics.
Chemicals, hormones and artificial yolk
colourants are not added to the chickens' food.
Our egg mayonnaise and even all our cakes
and muffins are made with free-range eggs.

Egg florentine baguette

BAGUETTE	½ baguette
FILLING	90 g (3¼ oz) egg mayo (see recipe on page 82)
	Pret seasoning (Basics, page 251)
	2–3 slices Italian matured cheese, such as parmesan or pecorino
	4 slices tomato
	4 rings red onion
	1 small onion, roughly chopped
	1 handful spinach leaves

CUT THE BAGUETTE almost in half lengthways (leaving one edge still attached) and spread the egg mayonnaise over the bottom half; using two forks works best. Sprinkle with the seasoning and arrange the cheese along the length of the baguette — it makes a great difference to the fun of eating if there is actually some cheese in both the first and the last bite, as well as those in between of course, so make sure you don't skimp. Arrange the tomato and onion on top of the cheese, then cram in some spinach leaves. Cover with the top half of the baguette, pressing down gently to keep everything in place.

Turkey, mustard and crispy onions baguette

BAGUETTE | ½ baguette
FILLING | 25 g (1 oz) mustard mayo (Basics, page 242)
| Pret seasoning (Basics, page 251)
| 15 g (½ oz) crispy onions (finely sliced and crisply fried)
| 60 g (2¼ oz) cooked turkey, sliced
| 4 slices tomato
| 1 handful rocket (arugula) leaves

SLICE THE BAGUETTE in half horizontally. Spread the mayo over the bottom half and sprinkle with seasoning. Distribute the onions over the mayo and then arrange the turkey slices on top. Place the tomato slices in a row on top of the turkey and then add the rocket. Replace the top of the baguette, pressing firmly to keep it in place.

CROISSANTS

Egg and bacon croissant

CROISSANT	1 croissant (straight, rather than crescent-shaped)
FILLING	25 g (1 oz) egg mayo (see recipe on page 82)
	2 rashers streaky bacon, grilled
	squirt of tomato ketchup
	Pret seasoning (Basics, page 251)

USING SCISSORS, CUT an opening from one end of the croissant to the other to form a pocket. Open out the croissant and spread the egg mayo right the way along the opening; using two forks works best. Slot the bacon in, squirt with ketchup and sprinkle seasoning over everything, bearing in mind that the bacon may be quite salty.

Ham and cheese croissant

CROISSANT	1 croissant
FILLING	2 slices hard cheese, such as greve, emmenthal or gruyère
	2–3 thin slices ham

SLICE OPEN THE CROISSANT horizontally. Position the slices of cheese overlapping on the bottom half of the croissant and the ham above. Close the croissant tightly. This could also be heated in a warm oven for about 10 minutes to melt the cheese.

Mushroom, cheese and walnut croissant

CROISSANT | 1 croissant
FILLING | 1 portobello mushroom, seasoned with pepper and grilled (broiled)
| for 5–7 minutes on each side (see Note)
| 1 slice gorgonzola cheese
| 10 g (¼ oz) walnuts or pecans
| 1 tbsp chopped chives

HEAT THE GRILL (broiler) to high. Slice the croissant in half horizontally, removing the top completely. Cut the mushroom in half and place the halves on the base of the croissant. Top with the cheese and walnuts. Place under the grill for about 3 minutes, until the crosissant is hot and the cheese is melted. Sprinkle the chives over the melted cheese and cover with the top of the croissant.

NOTE When seasoning the mushroom, do add some salt if you like, but be aware of the potential saltiness of the cheese before being too enthusiastic.

SANDWICHES

Making a sandwich tends to be something that one does for oneself, standing by the kitchen counter with the fridge door open and a knife in the hand. The sandwich is then eaten on the hoof or possibly taken to a quiet corner to be consumed in blissful isolation. It is probably comparatively quite rare that you would undertake sandwich making on the scale of Pret (and, if you do, please let us know how seriously you intend to compete!). So, when it comes to quantities the options are firstly, how much do you want to eat and secondly, what's in the fridge?

Writing recipes for sandwiches is a little like giving a set of instructions for tooth brushing. Everyone has their own way of doing it — the exact amount of toothpaste is really a matter of personal preference, as is the brushing sequence. With sandwich making we can give suggestions of combinations that have worked for us and offer hints of how to set about assembling those combinations, but as for a real recipe with rigid quantities, better not. Whilst we mention rather precise grams, ounces and spoonfuls, treat them as a guide in this section; where it matters that you use precise ratios is for sauces, cakes and biscuits (cookies), and don't worry, we'll dictate those most specifically. Over the next few pages, please feel constrained by no more than the recommendation for two slices of bread per sandwich — the rest is really up to you.

Chicken and yoghurt dressing

BREAD | 2 slices malted grain, rye or white bread
FILLING | salt and coarse-ground black pepper
50 g (1¾ oz) cooked chicken (see Note)
20 g (¾ oz) Pret yoghurt dressing (Basics, page 247)
1 lemon, freshly squeezed
4 red onion rings
5 slices cucumber
1 handful of rocket (arugula) leaves

SEASON THE FIRST SLICE of bread with salt and pepper. Slice the chicken into decent chunks and mix it with the yoghurt dressing. Spread the chicken mix over the seasoned bread. Squeeze lemon juice over the chicken mixture — we do it in a 'Z' shape to be sure to cover each corner and some of the middle too.

Place an onion ring in each corner of the sandwich. Place a slice of cucumber on top of the onion rings and one in the centre. Spread a handful of rocket over the whole sandwich and cover with the second slice of bread. Press gently to fix everything together. Slice and eat.

NOTE Any chicken is good for this sandwich. More often than not, people think that chicken breast is the best thing to use. It certainly looks good; pale and interesting with a smooth and even texture. But, try chicken thighs sometimes — they have so much more flavour and they won't be dry, while breast-meat often is.

Chicken caesar

BREAD	2 slices malted grain or garlic-toasted tomato bread
FILLING	salt and coarse-ground black pepper
	50 g (1¾ oz) cooked chicken (see Note)
	25 g (1 oz) caesar mayo (Basics, page 239)
	4 slices tomato
	1 handful mixed salad leaves

SEASON THE FIRST SLICE of bread with salt and pepper. Slice or shred (pulling it apart by hand) the chicken and mix it with the caesar mayo. Spread the chicken mix over the seasoned bread; using two forks works best.

Place a slice of tomato in each corner of the sandwich. Spread a handful of mixed salad leaves over the whole sandwich and cover with the second slice of bread. Press gently to fix everything together. Slice and eat.

NOTE Slicing the chicken is probably the most sensible way to cut it because the sandwich will then be easier to hold. If you opt for chunks instead, the whole thing might fall apart, unless you clamp the bread down hard over the filling and keep both hands on the task.

Chicken avocado

BREAD	2 slices malted grain, rye or wholemeal bread
FILLING	½ avocado
	25 g (1oz) real mayo (Basics, page 236)
	50 g (1¾ oz) cooked chicken
	salt and coarse-ground black pepper
	4 basil leaves
	1 handful mixed salad leaves

PEEL THE HALF AVOCADO by sliding a spoon between the flesh and skin and easing them apart. Cut the flesh into 5 mm (¼ in) slices. Arrange them on the first slice of bread. Using a spatula, spread the mayo gently over the avocado. If you have to interrupt the making of this sandwich, try to ensure that the mayo is covering the avocado — this will prevent it from turning brown, because of the vinegar in the mayo.

Cut the chicken into 5 mm (¼ in) slices and distribute evenly over the mayo. Season with salt and pepper.

Place a basil leaf in each corner of the sandwich. Spread the salad leaves over the whole sandwich and cover with the second slice of bread. Press gently to fix everything together. Slice and eat.

VARIATIONS There are so many options with this one: add some chilli sauce to the mayo; substitute tarragon for the basil; use spinach leaves instead of the mixed salad; add some bits of bacon and chopped spring onion; use leftover duck instead of chicken; sprinkle some worcestershire sauce over the avocado.

Coronation chicken

SAUCE	1 small onion, diced
	6 dried apricots, diced
	1 small green apple, diced
	1 tbsp raisins
	1 tsp sunflower oil
	1 tbsp mild curry powder
	$\frac{1}{2}$ lemon, freshly squeezed
	25 g (1 oz) real mayo (Basics, page 236)
BREAD	2 slices of malted grain or wholemeal (whole-wheat) bread
FILLING	50 g (1$\frac{3}{4}$ oz) cooked chicken, sliced or in chunks
	25 g (1 oz) mango chutney
	a sprinkling of flaked toasted almonds
	4 slices tomato
	salt and coarse-ground black pepper
	1 cos (romaine) lettuce leaf

TO MAKE THE SAUCE fry the onion, apricots, apple and raisins in the oil over medium heat for 7–8 minutes, or until beginning to brown. Add the curry powder and cook for 3 minutes, stirring well. Add 100 ml (3$\frac{1}{2}$ fl oz) water and simmer for 15 minutes, or until the apricots are soft. Keep a lid on and add more water if necessary, so that it doesn't dry out. Whizz everything up in a food processor until smooth and leave it to cool before adding the lemon juice and mayonnaise.

Mix the chicken with 1 tablespoon of the sauce. Spread the chicken mix over the first slice of bread. Spread the mango chutney over the chicken mixture and sprinkle over the almonds. Place a tomato slice in each corner of the sandwich. Season, top with the lettuce and second slice of bread. Press gently to fix everything together. Slice and eat.

NOTE Left-over sauce can be stored for about a week in the fridge in a tightly sealed jar.

⚜ PASSION FACT ⚜

Every Pret has its own kitchen. We don't have a factory.
We make our sandwiches, baguettes and wraps one by one, right
there, throughout the day. You won't find sell-by dates and storage
information on our sandwiches and wraps. At the end of the
day, we prefer to give to charity whatever we haven't sold. Not
only does this help to feed the homeless, but it also ensures
we don't compromise our standards.

Classic egg mayonnaise

BREAD	2 slices malted grain, rye or bloomer bread
FILLING	2 hardboiled eggs
	30 g (1 oz) real mayo (Basics, page 236)
	salt and coarse-ground black pepper
	1 teaspoon gherkin (pickle) and/or capers, chopped (optional)
	4 slices tomato (optional)
	1 handful mustard and cress or watercress

HAVING HARDBOILED THE EGGS for 10 minutes, immediately plunge them into cold water for about 5 minutes (this really makes a huge difference to the peeling). Peel the eggs (rinsing off any stray bits of shell — the crunch shell provides is not pleasant) and mash with a fork, adding the mayonnaise as you mash. If the eggs are too warm, the mayo might melt — it would still taste the same but it's the consistency that suffers — so either do the mashing with a knob of unsalted butter to help it along or twiddle your thumbs and take time selecting which slices of bread you will use, then mash away and season with salt and pepper. You could put everything into a food processor and whizz (or rather, use the 'pulse' or intermittent mode) for 5 seconds instead — but don't look away for even a nanosecond or you will find egg purée in the bowl when you turn back. It really is that quick. If you were thinking of being adventurous with the gherkins and/or capers, this would be the time to add them to the egg mixture.

Spread the egg mix over the first slice of bread. Place a tomato slice in each corner of the sandwich. Spread a handful of cress over the whole sandwich and cover with the second slice of bread. Press gently to fix everything together. Cut the sandwich into triangles — four small ones would be rather appealing — or you could be really dainty and, having removed the crusts, cut the sandwich into fingers.

If you want these sandwiches for a tea party (along with cucumber sandwiches and scones of course), they can be made reasonably well in advance (an hour or two) and kept fresh by covering the whole plate of sandwiches with a tea towel (an impeccably clean one) that has been put under the cold tap and then wrung out really well — the dampness will keep the sandwiches from drying out—but damp is the word, not soggy, so wring effectively, and be sure to tuck the edges of the cloth firmly around the plate to stop air and egg-sandwich pilferers from sneaking in. Cling film would be an alternative.

The principal ingredients of this recipe — hardboiled eggs and mayonnaise — are used (instead of the more traditional slices of egg that one might expect) in many of our other sandwiches and baguettes, even in the Pret staples 'Egg and bacon' or 'Egg and smoked salmon' breakfast baguettes and the hugely popular 'All day breakfast'. You could devise your own variations — we won't mind.

This recipe is the quantity for one sandwich, but multiply the recipe by adding only 1 egg (rather than 2) and 20 g (¾ oz) real mayo per extra sandwich.

Crayfish avocado

BREAD	2 slices malted grain or wholemeal bread
FILLING	½ avocado
	25 g (1 oz) 50:50 dressing (Basics, page 245)
	salt and coarse-ground black pepper
	60 g (2¼ oz) crayfish
	5 slices cucumber
	1 handful rocket (arugula) leaves

PEEL THE HALF AVOCADO and cut the flesh into 5 mm (¼ in) slices. Arrange them on the first slice of bread. Using a spatula, spread the dressing gently over the avocado. Season with salt and pepper. If you have to interrupt the making of this sandwich, try to ensure that the dressing is covering the avocado — this will prevent it from turning brown (because of the vinegar in the dressing).

Cut the crayfish into 5 mm (¼ in) slices. Distribute the crayfish evenly over the dressing. Place a cucumber slice in each corner of the sandwich and one in the centre. Spread a handful of rocket over the whole sandwich and cover with the second slice of bread. Press gently to fix everything together. Slice and eat.

Italian cheese avocado

BREAD | 2 slices malted grain, wholemeal or ciabatta bread
FILLING | ½ avocado
25 g (1 oz) real mayo (Basics, page 236)
salt and coarse-ground black pepper
2 tsp pine nuts
2–3 slices Italian matured cheese, such as parmesan or pecorino
1 handful mixed salad leaves
4 slices tomato
5 basil leaves

PEEL THE HALF AVOCADO and cut the flesh into 5 mm (¼ in) slices. Arrange them on the first slice of bread. Using a spatula, spread the mayo gently over the avocado. If you have to interrupt the making of this sandwich, try to ensure that the mayo is covering the avocado — this will prevent it from turning brown (because of the vinegar in the mayo). Season with salt and pepper and sprinkle with the pine nuts.

Arrange the slices of cheese evenly over the top. Place a tomato slice and basil leaf in each corner of the sandwich, with an extra basil leaf in the centre. Spread a handful of mixed salad leaves over the whole sandwich and cover with the second slice of bread. Press gently to fix everything together. Slice and eat.

VARIATIONS Try different cheeses with this sandwich, particularly creamy ones or, even better, creamy blue cheeses like dolcelatte or gorgonzola.

Roast beef and crispy onion

BREAD	2 slices malted grain bread
FILLING	30 g (1 oz) horseradish mayo (Basics, page 243)
	70 g (2½ oz) rare roast beef
	5 g (⅛ oz) crispy onions (either fried at home or bought)
	4 slow-roasted tomato quarters (Basics, page 249)
	½ handful each spinach leaves and watercress
	salt and coarse-ground black pepper

HOWEVER YOU PREFER your beef — some like layering flimsy slivers whilst others will prefer sturdy slabs — don't slice it until you are about to fling it into a closed sandwich, or the exposure to air will replace the attractive rosy pink colour with a dull grey. The flavour will remain juicy and rare, but looks are important.

Spread the horseradish mayo over the first slice of bread. Layer your perfectly sized beef slices lavishly across the base. Sprinkle with the onions and top with the tomatoes. Spread the spinach and watercress over the whole sandwich. If, by any chance, you are tempted to coat the dark green peppery leaves with a small amount of dressing — simply to gild perfection one stage further — then use a light balsamic and olive oil concoction, taking care to season with salt and black pepper. Cover with the second slice of bread. Press gently to fix everything together. Slice and eat.

VARIATION Another possible path to take would be to make your horseradish mayo with wasabi rather than traditional horseradish. If taking that route, we'd also suggest dabbing the beef with a little grated ginger (very finely so that you gather the juice rather than the fibrous root) and to swap the crispy onions for some exceedingly fine slices of spring onion (scallion). Having gone this far, it might be best to replace the sea salt with soy sauce — and if you could get hold of some chrysanthemum (shungiku) leaves, well, that really would be something — their slight bitterness is ideal with beef.

Big prawn and spinach

BREAD	2 slices malted grain or sourdough bread
FILLING	65 g (2¼ oz) peeled prawns (shrimp) (double the quantity if they have their shells on) (see Note)
	25 g (1 oz) real mayo (Basics, page 236)
	1 handful spinach leaves

IF YOU'VE SUCCEEDED in getting some fresh, uncooked prawns you can have great fun seasoning them with all sorts of interesting things: garlic, chilli, cardamom, coriander — some, or even all of them actually. If they were pre-cooked, the seasoning can be mixed effectively into the mayonnaise or even sprinkled on top. With either type, check the flavour before adding seasoning — sometimes they are remarkably salty.

Fry the prawns in a little hot, seasoned oil for 2–3 minutes, or until they turn pink all over. If they are huge, they'll need a little longer to cook through — you can tell if they are properly cooked, as they'll lose their translucency. When the prawns have cooled, peel, devein if necessary, and cut them into chunky pieces so that they are a little easier to eat and to hold in place (not lengthways, that would take away the thrill of biting into the thick texture).

Spread the mayo over the first slice of bread. If the prawns were bought pre-cooked, spark them up a little now by mixing with chilli sauce or sprinkle some sauce directly onto the mayo. Layer the prawn chunks across the base. Spread a handful of spinach leaves over the whole sandwich and cover with the second slice of bread. Press gently to fix everything together. Slice and eat.

NOTE If buying peeled prawns, choose large ones for the best texture, and if you can possibly taste them, do, because the larger ones can often be flavourless. Be sure to drain them of any extra water by squeezing between sheets of kitchen paper.

❧ PASSION FACT ☙

New Pret ham comes from Farm Assured farms,
which guarantees the pigs are reared on a vegetarian diet.
The colour, texture and taste of our ham is a world apart from
the shiny, slippery, square stuff commonly found in most
sandwiches. All our hams are hand-glazed with honey and
cloves and then baked in the oven. As a final touch,
we now hand-trim 95 per cent of the fatty white bit —
leaving just enough to provide the perfect flavour.

Ham, cheese and mustard

BREAD	2 slices malted grain bread
FILLING	20 g (³/₄ oz) mustard mayo (Basics, page 242)
	Pret seasoning (Basics, page 251)
	55 g (2 oz) sliced ham
	2 slices greve, emmenthal or gruyère cheese
	4 slices tomato
	1 handful of mixed salad leaves

SPREAD THE MUSTARD MAYO over the first slice of bread and sprinkle with the seasoning. Arrange the slices of ham, cheese and tomato evenly over the top. Spread a handful of mixed salad leaves over the whole sandwich and cover with the second slice of bread. Press gently to fix everything together. Slice and eat.

Humous salad

BREAD	2 slices malted grain bread
FILLING	60 g (2¼ oz) humous (see recipe on page 169)
	Pret seasoning (Basics, page 251)
	5 slices cucumber
	2 rings red pepper (capsicum)
	1 handful mixed salad leaves

SPREAD THE HUMOUS over the first slice of bread and sprinkle with the seasoning. Place a cucumber slice in each corner and one in the centre of the sandwich. Add the pepper rings, slightly overlapping each other. Spread the salad leaves over the whole sandwich and cover with the second slice of bread. Press gently to fix everything together. Slice and eat.

★ THE LUNCH BOX ★ THE LUNCH BOX ★ THE LUNCH BOX

Mature cheddar

BREAD	2 slices malted grain bread
FILLING	15 g (1/2 oz) real mayo (Basics, page 236)
	Pret seasoning (Basics, page 251)
	25 g (1 oz) Pret pickle (Basics, page 248), or a brand such as Branston
	3–4 thin slices mature cheddar
	4 slices tomato
	4 rings red onion
	1 handful mixed salad leaves

SPREAD THE MAYO over the first slice of bread and sprinkle with the seasoning. Spread the pickle over the mayo. Evenly distribute the cheese slices on top and place a tomato slice and onion ring in each corner.

Spread the salad leaves over the whole sandwich and cover with the second slice of bread. Press gently to fix everything together. Slice and eat.

Classic tuna

BREAD	2 slices malted grain bread
FILLING	100 g (3½ oz) tuna mayo (Basics, page 241)
	5 slices cucumber
	Pret seasoning (Basics, page 251)
	1 handful mixed salad leaves

SPREAD THE TUNA MAYO over the first slice of bread; using two forks works best. Place a cucumber slice in each corner and one in the centre of the sandwich and sprinkle with the seasoning. Spread the salad leaves over the whole sandwich and cover with the second slice of bread. Press gently to fix everything together. Slice and eat.

This is one of the most spectacularly popular things we make — amazing to consider how many must have sold over the years. The filling can be put anywhere, sandwiches, wraps, baguettes, wherever you care to put it.

All day breakfast

BREAD	2 slices malted grain or wholemeal bread
FILLING	50 g (1¾ oz) egg mayo (see recipe on page 82)
	1 cooked sausage
	dollop of real mayo (Basics, page 236)
	4 rashers cooked bacon (see Note)
	good squirt of tomato ketchup
	4 slices tomato
	1 handful mustard and cress

SPREAD THE EGG MAYO on one slice of bread; using two forks works best. Slice the sausage lengthways into four strips if it is big enough, or simply slice in half if it's a skinny thing, and arrange on the bread. Spread the real mayo over the sausage slices — this time using a spatula. Arrange the bacon slices on top of the mayo.

Squeeze some ketchup across the top of the bacon — we do it in a 'figure-of-eight', which gives just the right amount, well distributed. Fit the tomato slices neatly over the four quarters of the sandwich and top with a generous helping of mustard and cress. Add the second slice of bread. Press gently to fix everything together. Slice and eat.

NOTE By using pre-cooked crispy bacon that is now available in many shops, this can be a pretty swift sandwich to assemble when you have some left-over breakfast sausages. The egg can be added in slices rather than making an egg mayo — but the sandwich will have a less voluptuous texture.

More than mozzarella

BREAD	2 slices malted grain bread
FILLING	15 g (½ oz) real mayo (Basics, page 236)
	1 tsp pine nuts, toasted
	4 slices tomato
	5 slices mozzarella
	a pinch of Maldon sea salt
	5 basil leaves
	1 handful of rocket (arugula) leaves

SPREAD THE MAYO over the first slice of bread. Sprinkle over the pine nuts and place a tomato slice in each corner of the sandwich. Top with the mozzarella slices and season with sea salt. Place a basil leaf in each corner and one in the centre of the sandwich. Spread the rocket leaves over the whole sandwich and cover with the second slice of bread. Press gently to fix everything together. Slice and eat.

Yummy yoghurt prawns

BREAD	2 slices malted grain bread
FILLING	30 g (1 oz) Pret yoghurt dressing (Basics, page 247)
	80 g (2¾ oz) cooked prawns (shrimp), peeled, deveined and squeezed dry
	4 slices tomato
	Pret seasoning (Basics, page 251)
	1 handful spinach leaves

CUT THE PRAWNS into chunks and mix with the yoghurt dressing. Spread the prawn mixture over the first slice of bread; using two forks works best. Place a tomato slice in each corner of the sandwich and sprinkle with the seasoning. Spread the spinach leaves over the whole sandwich and cover with the second slice of bread. Press gently to fix everything together. Slice and eat.

Egg, bacon and tomato

BREAD | 2 slices malted grain bread
FILLING | 90 g (3¼ oz) egg mayo (see recipe on page 82)
| Pret seasoning (Basics, page 251)
| 4 rashers bacon, cooked
| 5 roasted tomato quarters (Basics, page 249)
| 1 handful spinach leaves

SPREAD THE EGG MAYO on one slice of bread; using two forks works best. Sprinkle with the seasoning and top with the bacon. Place a tomato quarter in each corner of the sandwich and one in the centre. Add the spinach leaves and cover with the second slice of bread. Press gently to fix everything together. Slice and eat.

Smoked chicken, watercress and pickled walnuts

BREAD | 2 slices malted grain bread
FILLING | 25 g (1 oz) real mayo (Basics, page 236)
| 80 g (2¾ oz) smoked chicken, sliced
| 1 handful watercress, coated in a little French dressing
| 2 pickled walnuts, sliced

SPREAD THE MAYO over one slice of bread. Arrange the slices of chicken over the top and add the watercress. Distribute the walnut slices over the watercress. Top with the second slice of bread.

Smoked roast salmon and horseradish

BREAD	2 slices malted grain bread
FILLING	20 g ($^3/_4$ oz) horseradish mayo (Basics, page 243)
	Pret seasoning (Basics, page 251)
	80 g ($2^3/_4$ oz) smoked roast salmon
	4 slices cucumber
	1 handful rocket (arugula) leaves

SPREAD THE HORSERADISH MAYO over the first slice of bread and sprinkle with the seasoning. Top the mayo with the salmon, broken into uniform chunks, and place a cucumber slice in each corner of the sandwich. Spread the rocket leaves over the whole sandwich and cover with the second slice of bread. Press gently to fix everything together. Slice and eat.

We used to call this sandwich 'kippered' salmon but people seemed wary, so we changed the name and everyone seems to love it. Just goes to show how important a name is.

Smoked salmon and Gourmet salmon

SMOKED	2 thin slices white rye with caraway or wholemeal
	7 g (¼ oz) unsalted or slightly salted butter
	60 g (2¼ oz) smoked salmon, sliced
	a generous squirt of lemon juice
	Pret seasoning (Basics, page 251)
GOURMET	2 thin slices white rye with caraway or wholemeal
	20 g (¾ oz) Greek yoghurt
	2 tsp capers
	60 g (2¼ oz) smoked salmon, sliced
	a generous squirt of lemon juice
	salt and coarse-ground black pepper
	4 rings red onion
	1 handful mixed salad leaves

FOR EITHER VERSION, spread the butter or yoghurt over the first slice of bread. For the gourmet sandwich, add the capers at this stage. Spread the smoked salmon slices evenly over the bread, getting right to the edges. Squeeze a 'Z'-shape of lemon juice over the salmon and sprinkle with the seasoning. That's it for the simple version but for the gourmet one, add the onion rings, one in each corner, and spread the salad leaves over the whole sandwich. Cover with the second slice of bread. Press gently to fix everything together. Slice and eat.

VARIATIONS You could also add cream cheese to these sandwiches or perhaps some dill and mustard sauce and a few sprigs of dill weed. For ultimate refinement, take off the crusts and cut the sandwich into small squares or 'fingers'.

The difference between these two sandwiches is subtle and you could adapt the two versions into a third of your own creation.

We're fanatical about the salmon we put into your lunch.
In a Pret sandwich you will never find 'trimmings', nor will
you find salmon 'mash' and definitely no tinned stuff.
We poach our Scottish salmon one by one in great big
metal fish kettles with lemon juice and a little dill, which
adds to the flavour. We pick the bones out, often one at
a time, and carefully break off fat chunks ready
for our sandwiches.

Asparagus, aioli and artichoke hearts

ROLL	Malted grain roll
FILLING	25 g (1 oz) real mayo (Basics, page 236), with 1 clove crushed garlic added (aioli)
	6 asparagus spears, cooked
	2 marinated artichoke hearts, halved
	½ red pepper (capsicum), grilled (broiled)
	Pret seasoning (Basics, page 251)
	1 handful rocket (arugula) leaves
	1 tbsp balsamic vinegar
	1 tbsp grated parmesan

HAVING SPREAD THE GARLIC MAYO over the roll, pile the vegetables in a jumble, but make them stable enough that they do not all fall out with the first bite. Season, add the rocket and then sprinkle the balsamic vinegar and parmesan over everything before putting the other half of the roll on top.

VARIATION This combination would also work well in a hollowed baguette or a crusty roll, left for an hour or two for the flavours to mingle.

Pastrami on rye

BREAD	2 slices white rye with caraway
FILLING	20 g ($^3/_4$ oz) mustard mayo (Basics, page 242)
	Pret seasoning (Basics, page 251)
	1 gherkin (pickle), sliced
	50 g ($1^3/_4$ oz) pastrami, sliced
	4 rings red onion
	4 slices tomato
	1 handful mixed salad leaves

SPREAD THE MUSTARD MAYO over the first slice of bread and sprinkle with the seasoning. Top the mayo with the gherkin and pastrami and place an onion ring and tomato slice in each corner of the sandwich. Spread the salad leaves over the whole sandwich and cover with the second slice of bread. Press gently to fix everything together. Slice and eat.

Salt beef and horseradish

BREAD | 2 slices rye bread

FILLING | 7 g (¼ oz) unsalted butter

20 g (¾ oz) horseradish mayo (Basics, page 243)

Pret seasoning (Basics, page 251)

70 g (2½ oz) salt beef

4 rings red onion

4 slices tomato

1 handful spinach leaves

THIS IS ONE OF THE FEW sandwiches in which we use butter, rather than all mayo. Mustard mayo could be substituted for the horseradish mayo.

Spread the butter over both slices of bread — rye bread is particularly good with salt beef. Then spread the mayo over the first slice of bread and sprinkle with the seasoning. Top the mayo with the salt beef and place an onion ring and tomato slice in each corner of the sandwich. Spread the spinach leaves over the whole sandwich and cover with the second slice of bread. Press gently to fix everything together. Slice and eat.

★ THE LUNCH BOX ★ THE LUNCH BOX ★ THE LUNCH BOX

Chicken provençal

BREAD	2 slices malted grain bread
FILLING	20 g (³⁄₄ oz) caesar mayo (Basics, page 239)
	12 g (¹⁄₂ oz) pitted black olives
	55 g (2 oz) cooked chicken, sliced or shredded
	5 roasted tomato quarters (Basics, page 249)
	2 rings red pepper (capsicum)
	1 handful mixed salad leaves

SPREAD THE CAESAR MAYO over the first slice of bread and sprinkle the olives over. Top with the chicken and place a tomato quarter in each corner of the sandwich and one in the centre. Place the pepper rings overlapping each other diagonally across the top, then add the salad leaves and cover with the second slice of bread. Press gently to fix everything together. Slice and eat.

THE LUNCH BOX ★ THE LUNCH BOX ★ THE LUNCH BOX ★

⧢ PASSION FACT ⧢

Basil is high-maintenance. It's delicate. It bruises easily.
It would be so much easier just to use pesto sauce, but, alas,
we can't. We just love the taste of fresh basil too much.
So we order it in hand-picked bunches, have it delivered daily
and place it on our sandwiches one leaf at a time. Yes, the
demands of basil are great, but the rewards are even greater.

Chicken and basil salad

BREAD	2 slices malted grain bread
FILLING	25 g (1 oz) 50:50 dressing (Basics, page 245)
	10 g (¼ oz) pine nuts, toasted
	Pret seasoning (Basics, page 251)
	6 basil leaves
	4 slices tomato
	1 handful spinach leaves

SPREAD THE DRESSING over the first slice of bread, sprinkle over the pine nuts and seasoning. Position the basil leaves artistically over the top (not that they will be seen, but it is more fun whilst constructing to be a little flamboyant). Place a tomato slice in each corner, spread the spinach leaves over the whole sandwich and cover with the second slice of bread. Slice and eat.

Brie and cranberry

BREAD	2 slices malted grain bread
FILLING	15 g (½ oz) real mayo (Basics, page 236)
	Pret seasoning (Basics, page 251)
	50 g (1¾ oz) brie
	20 g (¾ oz) cranberry sauce
	10 g (¼ oz) pine nuts
	1 handful mixed salad leaves

SPREAD THE MAYO over the first slice of bread and sprinkle with the seasoning. Strategically position the brie so that it covers as much of the base as possible — you may need to do a little trimming to make best use of what's available. Using a teaspoon, spread the cranberry sauce over the cheese, then sprinkle with the pine nuts. Spread the mixed salad leaves over the whole sandwich and cover with the second slice of bread. Press gently to fix everything together. Slice and eat.

Pret Christmas lunch

BREAD	2 slices malted grain bread
FILLING	20 g ($^3/_4$ oz) real mayo (Basics, page 236)
	Pret seasoning (Basics, page 251)
	50 g (1$^3/_4$ oz) stuffing, sliced
	20 g ($^3/_4$ oz) cranberry sauce
	7 g ($^1/_4$ oz) crispy onions
	55 g (2 oz) cooked turkey, sliced or shredded
	1 handful spinach leaves

SPREAD THE MAYO over the first slice of bread and sprinkle with the seasoning. Arrange the stuffing across the bread, making sure that it reaches the corners, and spread it with the cranberry sauce. Sprinkle the onions all over and then add the turkey and spinach leaves and cover with the second slice of bread. Press gently to fix everything together. Slice and eat.

This is our answer to using the inevitable (and delicious) leftovers after Christmas lunch. Actually, there is no reason why you shouldn't start from scratch to create this as a sandwich, baguette or wrap (hot or cold), at any time of the year, not only as a lunch but for breakfast or supper or even a midnight feast. If you happen to have a few cold roasted potatoes or chipolata sausages lurking cheekily about, throw them in too. Brussels sprouts could replace the spinach leaves as the greenery (honestly, they could).

Ham and eggs bloomer

BREAD | 2 slices bloomer bread

FILLING | 20 g ($^3/_4$ oz) mustard mayo (Basics, page 242)

1 hardboiled egg, sliced

Pret seasoning (Basics, page 251)

60 g (2$^1/_4$ oz) ham, sliced

6 g ($^1/_8$ oz) Italian matured cheese, such as parmesan or pecorino,
    or matured cheddar, sliced

4 rings red onion

3 slices tomato

1 handful mixed salad leaves

SPREAD THE MUSTARD MAYO over the first slice of bread. We are very strict about edges being covered because it is jolly frustrating to have to munch through naked crusts before getting to the action. You may prefer to take care not to go beyond the edge in this particular sandwich — because the yellow of the mustard mayo can make the whole thing look a little unkempt if it is seeping beyond the boundaries — but up to the edges is a must.

Position the egg slices in two rows across the centre of the bread and sprinkle with the seasoning. Arrange the slices of ham and cheese on top, followed by a ring of onion in each corner and the tomato slices across the centre in a line. (This is certainly a chunky little sandwich!) Spread the salad leaves over the whole sandwich and cover with the second slice of bread. Press gently to fix everything together. Slice and eat.

Pastrami bloomer

BREAD	2 slices bloomer bread
FILLING	30 g (1 oz) mustard mayo (Basics, 242)
	Pret seasoning (Basics, page 251)
	1 gherkin (pickle), sliced
	50 g (1$\frac{3}{4}$ oz) pastrami, sliced
	4 rings red onion
	3 slices tomato
	1 handful mixed salad leaves

SPREAD THE MUSTARD MAYO over the first slice of bread and sprinkle with the seasoning. Top the mayo with the gherkin and pastrami and place an onion ring in each corner. Place the tomato slices diagonally across the top. Spread the salad leaves over the whole sandwich and cover with the second slice of bread. Press gently to fix everything together. Slice and eat.

NOTE You may notice that, apart from increasing the quantity of mayo and removing one slice of tomato, it is only the bread that makes this a different sandwich from the one on page 101. So here is an opportunity for research — try them both and see which of the two appeals most.

Smoked salmon and egg

BREAD	2 slices malted grain bread
FILLING	50 g (1¾ oz) egg mayo (see recipe on page 82)
	Pret seasoning (Basics, page 251)
	4 rings red onion
	45 g (1½ oz) smoked salmon, sliced
	1 handful spinach leaves

SPREAD THE EGG MAYO over one slice of bread; using two forks works best. Sprinkle with seasoning. Place an onion ring in each corner and then top with the smoked salmon, making sure that the slices of salmon reach the edges of the sandwich. Add the spinach leaves and the second slice of bread.

Lamb, redcurrant jelly and aubergine

BREAD	2 slices malted grain bread
FILLING	25 g (1 oz) real mayo (Basics, page 236)
	80 g (2¾ oz) lamb, cooked and trimmed of any fat, sliced
	1 tbsp redcurrant jelly mixed with 1 tsp balsamic vinegar
	2 slices aubergine (eggplant), grilled (broiled)
	Pret seasoning (Basics, page 251)
	1 handful spinach leaves

SPREAD THE MAYO over one slice of bread before arranging the lamb and the jelly on top. Arrange the aubergine across the meat and season well. Add the spinach leaves and the second slice of bread.

Ricotta, pesto, tomato and rocket

BREAD | 2 slices malted grain bread
FILLING | 80 g (2¾ oz) ricotta or cottage cheese
| 1 tbsp pesto (Basics, page 247)
| ½ tsp freshly grated lemon zest
| 4 slices tomato
| Pret seasoning (Basics, page 251)
| 1 handful rocket (arugula) leaves

SPREAD THE RICOTTA over one slice of bread and then add the pesto. This may be hard to spread evenly, so just make sure that there is a relatively even coverage dolloped strategically. Sprinkle the lemon zest and add a tomato slice to each corner. Season and add the rocket. Top with the second slice of bread.

Salami, cream cheese and olive

BREAD	2 slices malted grain bread
FILLING	30 g (1 oz) soft cream cheese
	5 slices milano or napoli salami
	10 g (¼ oz) pitted black olives, chopped
	4 slices tomato or red pepper (capsicum) or both
	2 tsp balsamic vinegar
	2 cos (romaine) lettuce leaves, chopped

SPREAD THE CREAM CHEESE over one slice of bread. Arrange the salami slices in each corner and one in the middle of the sandwich. Sprinkle the chopped olives over the top and then add the tomato or red pepper slices, again in each corner. Dab or sprinkle the balsamic vinegar over the surface. Pile the lettuce on top and add the second slice of bread.

Tuna St Tropez

BREAD	2 slices malted grain bread
FILLING	70 g (2½ oz) tuna mayo (Basics, page 241)
	10 g (¼ oz) capers
	1 hardboiled egg, sliced
	4 rings red onion
	4 slices tomato
	1 handful spinach leaves

SPREAD THE TUNA MAYO on one slice of bread; using two forks works best. Sprinkle over the capers and arrange the slices of egg over the top. Place an onion ring and tomato slice in each corner of the sandwich. Spread the spinach leaves over the whole sandwich and cover with the second slice of bread. Press gently to fix everything together. Slice and eat.

WRAPS

Tortilla wraps are delicious cold and fantastic hot. Cold wrapping is a good way of carting a salad about without a bowl, whilst by enveloping ingredients that improve when warmed, you have the most perfect way of transporting what amounts to a rolled-up pizza. All the melty cheese toppings that you might put on a pizza can go into a wrap and be carried to the touchline of a rugby match or be munched at a freezing bus stop. (If your thermos flask opening is wide enough, you might even be able to stuff the brown paper package inside to keep warm — but make sure that it will fit before you have a go.)

The wrapping process would be the same for all fillings, the only aspects you need to consider when making your own inventions are whether there is likely to be too much liquid that might start to drip out (over your shoes) and how long to heat the wrap. For most things, a hot oven (200°C/400°F/Gas 6) should be fine and the wrap should be in for at least 15 minutes so that the filling will be heated right through to the centre — any less and you run the risk of bacteria breeding in a jolly impressive way, which would be distinctly dangerous if the wrap were not eaten instantly. So, it's better to err on the side of overcooking.

Wrapping technique is the same for hot as for cold: tortilla flat on a surface; ingredients across one half; seasoning sprinkled over the whole surface; and roll up tightly. Whereas the cold wrap would at this point be cut in half (at an attractive slant), the hot one stays in one piece and is then rolled into a protective sheet of baking parchment, greaseproof paper or sturdy brown paper and tied with a length of string. Pop the parcel into the oven at the temperature mentioned above for 15 minutes (longer if you started with chilly ingredients or if you have thrown a large number into the oven at the same time, because the temperature of the oven will drop and take a while to recover). Once you remove it, tear the top half of the paper to expose the wrap and eat it like a lollipop. Do watch out for drips on shoes at this point — just in case.

For a party make some mini ones. Adjust the filling quantities but make sure that the flavour is very exciting (as if you wouldn't) and that the contents are not too dry because, with a smaller amount inside, the tortilla itself could predominate and seem a bit dull and chewy. You could of course use Vietnamese rice wraps, which can also be served hot or cold, but be careful as they are more delicate to wrap in miniature.

NEW WRAPS

Pret recently launched Hot Wraps as the most exciting contribution to hot food (on the move). Here is the way Simon Hargraves, Commercial Director (and performer extraordinaire) announced the new range to an audience of 400 Pret Shop Managers and Team Leaders at Pret's Quarter Brief in July 2006. The lights were dimmed and soft music started to play; one by one images appeared on the giant screen behind Simon as he (somewhat seductively) told the story that follows …

'It is with great joy that I stand before you and say: "We launch hot food in September!" Yes my friends, hot wraps are coming … At last, real hot food for Pret A Manger. But just why has it taken so long? There are hundreds of hot food choices we could have made. Pies and pasties. Ciabattas and paninis. Sausage rolls and pizza. We've considered them all and even tested a few. But nothing could live up to the real values of Pret Food. Twenty years of natural, preservative-free, handmade delicious food. Nothing was Pret Perfect — so many we tried were commodity products, stuff you could buy just anywhere. Remember Pret isn't a shop to pop into simply to get something to eat, Pret is a bit of an experience. Now we've got it! We've been testing Hot Wraps since August 2005. The results have been good. Over the trial we've tweaked recipes, tested new recipes and flavours, changed prices and carefully watched the sales. We think we've got it right. Here's our new baby … why is it so perfect?' (Lights lowered further, music becomes softer … Simon's voice lowers a few notches …)

'This is not just an ordinary piece of brown paper, this is a Pret A Manger, environmentally friendly, 100% recyclable piece of brown paper with the words "eat me like a lollipop" written on the side. This is not just any ordinary tortilla wrap, this is an authentic, hand-scorched, trans-fat free, 100% flour tortilla wrap gently encasing hand-cut crisp, red peppers, tender strips of starch-free plump chicken breast marinated in white wine, herbs and juniper berries. This is not just any red chilli sauce, this is a genuine Mexicano, jalapeño red tomato chilli sauce, just hot enough to tingle on your tongue but not too hot to blow your balls off.'

'This is not just food … this is Pret A Manger food.'

Tuna niçoise wrap

WRAP	1 tortilla wrap
FILLING	25 g (1 oz) 50:50 dressing (Basics, page 245)
	50 g (1¾ oz) tinned tuna, drained
	10 g (¼ oz) pitted black olives, sliced
	10 g (¼ oz) capers
	Pret seasoning (Basics, page 251)
	1 hardboiled egg, sliced
	3 slices tomato
	3 rings red onion
	1 handful spinach leaves

MIX THE DRESSING with the tuna and spread it over half of the wrap. Put the olives and capers in a line across the centre of the wrap, sprinkle with the seasoning and top with the egg slices, then the tomato, onion rings and finally the spinach. Roll up the wrap tightly and cut in half at an oblique angle — to look attractive and to make the first bite less awkward.

★ THE LUNCH BOX ★ THE LUNCH BOX ★ THE LUNCH BOX

Avocado wrap

WRAP	1 tortilla wrap
FILLING	20 g (¾ oz) 50:50 dressing (Basics, page 245)
	½ avocado
	7 g (¼ oz) toasted pine nuts
	Pret seasoning (Basics, page 251)
	1 handful spinach leaves
	3 slices tomato
	8 g (¼ oz) Italian matured cheese, such as parmesan or pecorino, sliced
	10 cm (4 in) long stick of cucumber
	7 basil leaves

SPREAD THE DRESSING over half the wrap. Slice the avocado and put it in a line across the centre of the wrap. Sprinkle the pine nuts and seasoning over the avocado. Top with the spinach, tomato and cheese slices, followed by the cucumber and basil. Roll up the wrap tightly and cut in half at an oblique angle — to look attractive and to make the first bite less awkward.

THE LUNCH BOX ★ THE LUNCH BOX ★ THE LUNCH BOX ★

Chop Chop. It takes three months to slice our vegetables. Sounds mad but that's how long we train our people before they're able to get chopping. This means they're super-fast, scarily accurate and can spot a badly sliced vegetable at 500 paces. Only then are they let loose on the tomatoes, peppers and cucumbers.

Serrano ham and basil in omelette wrap

WRAP	1 egg
	2 tsp cold water
	salt and coarse-ground black pepper
	1 tbsp very finely chopped chives or spring onion (scallion)
FILLING	1 tbsp crème fraîche
	3 slices serrano ham or prosciutto
	5 basil leaves

MIX THE EGG WITH THE WATER, salt and pepper and chives (or spring onion). Heat a non-stick frying pan gently — it shouldn't be too hot, the egg should set rather than fry — and using a ladle (prevents drips everywhere) pour in enough egg just to coat the bottom of the pan. The wrap needs to be thin or it will be difficult to roll into an elegant shape. Keep the heat low.

When it has set — try shaking the pan; the omelette is ready when it slides from side to side — turn it over (this is best done delicately with your fingers rather than aerodynamic manoeuvres) and let it heat a little more on the second side.

Slide the egg out of the pan onto a wooden board. You could use a plate, but the board will allow the steam to escape more effectively and prevent the egg from becoming soggy.

When the egg is cold — for this particular filling it needs to be cold, but for others (mozzarella and roasted tomato, for instance) it would be fine (a bonus) for there to be some warmth — spread the crème fraîche over one side, add the ham and basil leaves, making sure that some leaf appears at either end and also strategically positioned near the middle so that it will show brightly when assembled and cut. Roll up like a fat cigar. Cut in half diagonally (it looks better) and eat.

NOTE By making a very thin one-egg omelette in a non-stick pan, you have the ideal no-bread wrap that can be filled with anything. The non-stick aspect is key because if one has to use oil or butter to prevent sticking in the pan, the oiliness makes it less appealing to pick up and eat like an ordinary wrap. Make sure you season the omelette well — nothing worse than a bland outer layer — but bear in mind that the serrano ham will be salty.

Chicken salad wrap

WRAP | 1 tortilla wrap
FILLING | 20 g (¾ oz) 50:50 dressing (Basics, page 245)
| 20 g (¾ oz) rocket (arugula) leaves
| 55 g (2 oz) cooked chicken, sliced
| 3 slices tomato
| 2 rings red pepper (capsicum), cut in half
| 10 cm (4 in) long stick of cucumber
| Pret seasoning (Basics, page 251)

SPREAD THE DRESSING over half the wrap. Position the rocket leaves in a line across the centre and place the other ingredients on top. Season, roll up the wrap tightly and cut in half at an oblique angle.

Hoisin duck wrap

WRAP | 1 tortilla wrap
FILLING | 20 g (¾ oz) hoisin sauce
| 50 g (1¾ oz) roast duck (leg meat is best), shredded
| 8 rings red onion, cut in half
| 10 cm (4 in) long stick of cucumber
| 1 handful spinach leaves

SPREAD THE HOISIN SAUCE over half the wrap. Dollop the hoisin sauce in a line across the middle, followed by the duck, onion, cucumber and spinach leaves. Roll up the wrap tightly and cut in half at an oblique angle.

Jalapeño chicken hot wrap

WRAP	1 tortilla wrap
FILLING	½ cooked chicken breast, sliced
	4 slow-roasted tomato quarters (Basics, page 249)
	1 tsp chopped pickled green jalapeño chilli
	2 slices red pepper (capsicum)
	10 fine green beans, cooked in boiling water for 2 minutes
	squirt of tomato ketchup
	salt and coarse-ground black pepper
	2 slices greve, emmenthal or gruyère cheese

PREHEAT THE OVEN to 200°C (400°F/Gas 6). Place the wrap flat on a surface. Arrange the chicken pieces over one half of the wrap. Top with the tomato pieces, jalapeño, red pepper and beans. Squirt some ketchup across the centre of the wrap and season with salt and pepper. Finish with the cheese slices and roll the wrap across the filling and tightly into a long cigar.

To wrap the tortilla in paper, you'll need 1 piece of baking parchment, greaseproof paper or brown paper lined with greaseproof (looks quite smart), which is big enough to cover the whole wrap and turn in the sides. Do the same rolling technique as when filling the wrap but with the sides turned in to make it more like an envelope (this will stop the filling from wandering out when it is warm and runny, so it's quite important). Tie kitchen string round the middle, if possible including the turned-in edges.

Put in the preheated oven for 15 minutes. Take out and tear the paper from around one end so that you can eat the glorious, hot, runny, spicy chicken treat just like a lollipop (sort of).

Hot salt beef wrap

WRAP	1 tortilla wrap
FILLING	2 squirts of French's mustard
	100 g (3½ oz) salt beef or pastrami
	1 tbsp sauerkraut
	2 long slices pickled cucumber
	2 slices greve, emmenthal or gruyère cheese
	coarse-ground black pepper

PREHEAT THE OVEN to 200°C (400°F/Gas 6). Put the wrap on a flat surface. Squirt a 'Z'-shape of mustard on the half nearest to you. Arrange the salt beef on top and then the sauerkraut. Spread the cucumber slices on top of the sauerkraut and add a second squirt of mustard. Finally top with the cheese and season with pepper (not salt, because it'll be quite salty enough). Roll the wrap across the filling and tightly into a long cigar.

To wrap the tortilla in paper, you'll need 1 piece of baking parchment, greaseproof paper or brown paper lined with greaseproof (looks quite smart), which is big enough to cover the whole wrap and turn in the sides. Do the same rolling technique as when filling the wrap but with the sides turned in to make it more like an envelope (this will stop the filling from wandering out when it is warm and runny, so it's quite important). Tie string round the middle, if possible including the turned-in edges.

Put in the preheated oven for 15 minutes. Take out and tear the paper from around one end so that you can eat the wrap just like a lollipop (sort of).

Wraps are so versatile, you can fill them with whatever takes your fancy (within reason, or course). Here's a quick selection of some hot wrap filling ideas:

★ Beano's brunch: bacon, egg mayo, baked beans, sausage, cheddar cheese.

★ Salmon fishcake: poached or hot-smoked salmon on top of creamy mashed potato and a sprinkling of frozen peas — probably best to boil the peas for 3 minutes, drain them and then add to the wrap. A squeeze of lemon juice might also be a good addition. Make sure that the potato is well seasoned and not too dry. A couple of slices of greve, emmenthal or gruyère cheese could also be added to this wrap, but it shouldn't really be necessary if the potato is creamy enough.

★ Bangers and mash: leftover sausages and mashed potato with a spoonful of orange marmalade, some tomato quarters and lots of black pepper.

★ Bubble and squeak: mashed potato, savoy cabbage, cheese and lots of black pepper.

★ Christmas wrap: puréed parsnip and swede (rutabaga), turkey, chestnuts, stuffing, cranberry sauce and some raw red onion rings for crunch.

SALADS

Virtually every shop in the country now stocks pre-washed, bagged salad leaves. Only ten years ago it seemed outrageous to believe that anyone would be so lazy as to skive off lettuce-washing duty, particularly as the only stuff that was available in such clinical profligacy was iceberg lettuce. Now everything is pre-washed, gas-flushed and bagged in ever more whackily themed combinations. What about lettuce-flavoured lettuce, you know, the leaves that tasted of something? It has even become hard to find them with mud and insects all over them, and we have to pay silly sums to eat the vegetable-equivalent of blotting paper, which is all it is, a soak-all for salad dressing so that you don't actually have to drink it.

Enough ranting. What do we do about it? We hope that you will feel that our salad leaves are real and interesting, with enough variety in colour and texture to give your mouth (and mind) something to chew over. We have hand-picked them, so to speak, having had long conversations with our grower about the ideal combinations.

The other vegetables we use in our salads — like sugar snap peas, baby plum (roma) tomatoes or red peppers (capsicums) — are also carefully selected for their flavour and their texture, and we hope it shows.

When combining your salads, remember not to add dressing until you are about to eat. Although there are attractions about salad leftovers (see page 22), it would seem to make sense for everything to be looking bright and perky (rather than totally done-in) on the first outing.

Similarly, if the salad is to include cooked ingredients, such as bacon, chicken or hardboiled egg, make sure that they are cold before putting them anywhere near the leaves. Any warmth will create the same effect of exhaustion as an early-added dressing. There are times (and it was quite fashionable for a while) to serve *salades tièdes* (lukewarm salads) but they have to look as though the floppiness is absolutely intentional.

If you can, vary the types of lettuce and herbs as well as the other veg you use in a salad. It used to be thought that a salad should consist of lettuce, cucumber, tomato and pickled beetroot with a pale squirt of salad cream put on the plate next to (but not touching) everything else. We have come a long way from that perception, but a greater sense of adventure could still be encouraged.

The dressing you use will largely depend on personal preference and there are a couple of recipes in the book — French dressing and sweet chilli dressing (Basics, pages 244–247). But, you know you can use any of the mayonnaise recipes as a base and dilute them with some vinegar, lemon or lime juice or even a spot of yoghurt — just to make them a little less heavy. You could also make a dressing out of guacamole or humous or blend some blue cheese with the basic French dressing.

Simple tuna
Serves 1

SALAD

70 g (2½ oz) mixed salad leaves

80 g (2¾ oz) tinned tuna, well drained

4 baby plum (roma) tomatoes

1 hardboiled egg, cut in half horizontally

10 g (¼ oz) pitted black olives, sliced

10 g (¼ oz) capers

30 g (1 oz) sugar snap peas, uncooked

Pret seasoning (Basics, page 251)

3 rings red onion

2 tbsp French dressing (Basics, page 245)

FOR THE PRET WAY, put the leaves in a bowl. Arrange the tuna on one side of the bowl and the tomatoes dotted about. Put one egg half on each side of the tuna and sprinkle the olives and capers over the top. Put the sugar snaps opposite the tuna and sprinkle seasoning over everything. Arrange the onion rings on top and serve with the dressing.

Tuna niçoise
Serves 2

DRESSING	1 tbsp red wine vinegar
	a squeeze of lemon juice
	salt and coarse-ground black pepper
	1 small clove garlic, finely chopped
	1 tsp fresh thyme leaves, finely chopped
	1 tsp fresh chervil leaves, finely chopped
	½ tsp dijon mustard
	3 tbsp olive oil
SALAD	½ cos (romaine) lettuce, torn into 6 cm (2½ in) strips (no measuring needed)
	4 new potatoes, boiled and sliced
	150 g (5½ oz) green beans, cooked
	10 baby plum (roma) tomatoes, halved
	200 g (7 oz) tuna, grilled (broiled), or tinned in brine if fresh is not available
	2 hardboiled eggs, quartered
	4 anchovy fillets, sliced lengthways
	1 large handful pitted black olives
	1 handful flat-leaf parsley, roughly chopped
	a sprinkling of capers or chopped caperberries

PUT ALL THE DRESSING ingredients, apart from the oil, in a bowl and beat with a fork. Add the oil and whisk again. When making any oil-based dressing it is a good idea to combine all the other ingredients first and to add the oil last. The oil will coat all the seasonings with a waterproof film, acting as a barrier to effective mingling.

Arrange the salad ingredients in a wide bowl (more artistic potential over a larger area) starting with the lettuce and potatoes and finishing with the more delicate ingredients on top. Pour the dressing (having given it a last-minute whisking) over the whole salad and serve.

Alfresco chicken
Serves 1

SALAD | 55 g (2 oz) chicken, cooked, sliced or in chunks
25 g (1 oz) Pret yoghurt dressing (Basics, page 247)
70 g (2½ oz) mixed salad leaves
10 g (¼ oz) pitted black olives, sliced
3 rings red pepper (capsicum), cut in quarters
10 g (¼ oz) pine nuts, toasted
Pret seasoning (Basics, page 251)
2 tbsp French dressing (Basics, page 245)

MIX THE CHICKEN with the yoghurt dressing. Put the salad leaves in a bowl and arrange the other ingredients decoratively on top, adding the pine nuts last. Sprinkle with the seasoning and serve with the French dressing.

Chicken avocado
Serves 1

SALAD | 55 g (2 oz) chicken, cooked, sliced or in chunks

25 g (1 oz) Pret yoghurt dressing (Basics, page 247)

70 g (2½ oz) mixed salad leaves

5 roasted tomato quarters (Basics, page 249)

10 g (¼ oz) pitted black olives, sliced

3 rings red onion

½ avocado, sliced

lemon juice, to squeeze over the avocado slices

1 handful mustard and cress

Pret seasoning (Basics, page 251)

2 tbsp French dressing (Basics, page 245)

MIX THE CHICKEN with the yoghurt dressing. Put the leaves into a bowl and distribute everything over the top, finishing with the mustard and cress. Sprinkle with the seasoning and serve with the French dressing.

Basil, pasta and French dressing
Serves 1

SALAD | 146 g (5¼ oz) cooked pasta, cold
25 g (1 oz) fresh herb mayo (Basics, page 238)
40 g (1½ oz) mixed salad leaves
4 baby plum (roma) tomatoes
10 basil leaves
7 g (¼ oz) pine nuts
8 g (¼ oz) Italian matured cheese, such as parmesan or pecorino, in small pieces
Pret seasoning (Basics, page 251)
2 tbsp French dressing (Basics, page 245)

MIX THE PASTA with the herb mayo. Put the salad leaves in a bowl and the pasta next to them. Add the tomatoes, basil and pine nuts. Put the cheese on top, sprinkle with the seasoning and serve with the dressing.

Humous and feta
Serves 1

SALAD | 70 g (2½ oz) mixed salad leaves
60 g (2¼ oz) humous (see recipe on page 169)
3 baby plum (roma) tomatoes
50 g (1¾ oz) feta, crumbled
½ tortilla wrap, rolled
Pret seasoning (Basics, page 251)
5 rings red onion
2 tbsp French dressing (Basics, page 245)

PUT THE SALAD LEAVES in a bowl. Add the humous in a scoop at one side of the bowl and the tomatoes next to it. Arrange the feta opposite the humous and the rolled tortilla between the two. Sprinkle the seasoning over everything. Position the onion rings on top and serve with the dressing.

Crayfish and smoked salmon
Serves 1

SALAD

70 g (2½ oz) mixed salad leaves

40 g (1½ oz) smoked salmon, finely sliced

50 g (1¾ oz) crayfish, well drained

Pret seasoning (Basics, page 251)

5 slices cucumber

1 wedge of lemon, for squeezing over

2 tbsp sweet chilli dressing (Basics, page 246)

PUT THE SALAD LEAVES in a bowl. Arrange the salmon on top, on one side, and the crayfish opposite. Sprinkle the seasoning over and arrange the cucumber slices and lemon wedge on top. Serve with the dressing.

Carrot, chilli and walnut
Serves 2

SALAD

2 tbsp sweet chilli dressing (Basics, page 246)

2 tbsp walnut oil

1 tbsp white wine vinegar

350 g (12 oz) grated carrot

Pret seasoning (Basics, page 251)

1 handful walnuts

MAKE THE DRESSING by mixing the chilli dressing, walnut oil and vinegar together. Pour over the grated carrot and season. Add the walnuts. Leave to stand for about an hour, if possible, because it really helps the flavours to develop. If the time isn't available, however, make a stronger dressing.

Pret tabbouleh
Serves 1

SALAD	2 tbsp reconstituted Israeli couscous (according to packet instructions)
	1 tbsp cooked peas
	1 tbsp cooked broad beans
	1 tbsp cooked puy lentils
	1 tbsp fried, diced pancetta, lardons or bacon
	$\frac{1}{2}$ tbsp finely diced red onion
	$\frac{1}{2}$ tbsp finely sliced spring onion (scallion)
	$\frac{1}{2}$ tbsp finely chopped flat-leaf parsley
	$\frac{1}{4}$ tbsp finely chopped mint
DRESSING	juice and zest of $\frac{1}{2}$–1 lemon (depending on the juiciness)
	1 tsp finely crushed garlic
	salt and coarse-ground black pepper
	1 tbsp olive oil

ASSEMBLE AND MIX all the salad ingredients in a large bowl. Make the dressing by adding the lemon juice and zest to the garlic and seasoning and then whisking in the oil. Add the dressing to the bowl of couscous, vegetables, pancetta and herbs.

NOTE This salad can be made quite a number of hours before serving — the flavours merge and settle into one another in the most glorious way. If you taste it to check the seasoning whilst you are mixing it, you'll find it hard not to continue taste-testing over and over again, but it is worth leaving some to eat later. Serve on its own or with some cold, sliced chicken or even some salmon or smoked mackerel.

Steak, rocket and balsamic vinegar
Serves 2

SALAD	1 large lean steak (about 180 g/6 oz), rib eye for best flavour, grilled rare
	2 large handfuls rocket (arugula) leaves
	shavings of parmesan or pecorino cheese
DRESSING	2 tbsp balsamic vinegar
	1 tbsp dijon mustard
	salt and coarse-ground black pepper
	2 tbsp olive oil

TRIM THE STEAK of excess fat and slice into 5 mm (¼ in) strips. Put the leaves into a bowl and arrange the steak strips on top. Mix the dressing ingredients together, adding the oil last. Pour the dressing all over the steak — it will run down into the rocket leaves. Scatter the parmesan shavings over the top and serve.

Prawn and rice noodle
Serves 2

SALAD

1 tbsp sesame oil

1 clove garlic, crushed

6 baby corn on the cob, sliced lengthways

1 red pepper (capsicum), very finely sliced

300 g (10½ oz) small prawns (shrimp), cooked

2 spring onions (scallions), finely sliced

150 g (5½ oz) rice noodles, cooked (you can also use glass/mung bean noodles or vermicelli)

75 ml (2½ fl oz) sweet chilli dressing (Basics, page 246)

1 large handful chopped coriander (cilantro) leaves

HEAT THE OIL in a frying pan over high heat and add the garlic. Fry for a minute and then add the corn and red pepper. Cook for 5 minutes, or until slightly softened but still with a slight crunch. Remove from the heat and allow to cool. When the vegetables are cold, add the remaining ingredients, apart from the coriander, and mix together well. Top with the coriander and serve.

Fennel, prawn and lime
Serves 2

SALAD	1 tbsp chopped mint
	1 tbsp chopped dill
	Pret seasoning (Basics, page 251)
	1 tbsp real mayo (Basics, page 236)
	1 tbsp crème fraîche
	1 lime, juice and zest
	1 fennel bulb, finely sliced
	250 g (9 oz) peeled, cooked prawns (shrimp) (see Note)
	2–3 spring onions (scallions), finely sliced

IN A BOWL, MIX TOGETHER the herbs, seasoning, mayo, crème fraîche, lime juice and zest. Add the fennel, prawns and spring onion, mix well and leave to stand for at least 30 minutes for the flavours to blend. Serve as a first course or to accompany a fish course. The mixture would also go very well in a sandwich.

NOTE Ensure the prawns are not too watery — squeeze them well if they are, or they will dilute the dressing.

★ THE LUNCH BOX ★ THE LUNCH BOX ★ THE LUNCH BOX

Wild mushroom, pine nut and watercress
Serves 2

SALAD

1 clove garlic, finely chopped

1 tbsp olive oil

100 g (3½ oz) wild mushrooms (any combination)

Pret seasoning (Basics, page 251)

10 g (¼ oz) pine nuts, toasted

1 hardboiled egg, quartered

2 large handfuls watercress

2 tbsp French dressing (Basics, page 245)

2 spring onions (scallions), cut into fine, long slivers

FRY THE GARLIC IN OIL and when beginning to brown, add the mushrooms. Keep the heat high so that any water released from the mushrooms evaporates instantly (wild mushrooms are less likely to be holding water than the cultivated varieties). When soft and well cooked, season well and allow to cool.

Add the pine nuts and hardboiled egg to the watercress and pour the French dressing over. Gently mix to coat with the dressing. Put the mushrooms on top of the salad and then add the fine shards of spring onion for colour and decoration.

THE LUNCH BOX ★ THE LUNCH BOX ★ THE LUNCH BOX ★

Wild rice and salmon
Serves 2

SALAD | 250 g (9 oz) wild rice, cooked and chilled (or a mixture of wild and
long-grain white rice would be fine too)
200 g (7 oz) salmon, cooked, chilled and broken into flakes
masses of finely chopped flat-leaf parsley
2 limes, juice and zest
salt and coarse-ground black pepper
huge handful of finely chopped spring onion (scallion)
100 ml (3½ fl oz) single (whipping) cream

GENTLY COMBINE ALL the ingredients, leaving the cream until the very last. The flavour of the lime will be absorbed very quickly and you may find that you need to add a little more for the taste to come through. Don't stint on the black pepper.

NOTE This is a cold version of a variation on the theme of kedgeree and of course could be made with other types of fish, for example, cod or smoked cod or haddock.

White cabbage, crispy noodle and sesame
Serves 2

SALAD | 100 g (3½ oz) rice noodles
oil, for frying
1 tbsp rice vinegar
1 tbsp fish sauce (nam pla)
1 tsp chilli flakes
1 clove garlic, crushed
1 tbsp sesame oil
1 tbsp sunflower oil
200 g (7 oz) white cabbage, finely shredded
20 g (¾ oz) sesame seeds, toasted

THE RICE NOODLES should be deep-fried to puff them up (rather like rice crispies), but you will be able to achieve the same effect in shallow oil by turning them over mid-fry. Keep the oil hot enough to prevent the noodles absorbing it, but not so wild that it frazzles and colours them. Drain them on kitchen paper and allow to cool before adding to the salad — so that they don't burn your mouth.

Mix together the rice vinegar, fish sauce, chilli flakes and garlic and leave to stand for 10 minutes for the chilli flavour to penetrate the liquids. Add the sesame and sunflower oils to the chilli vinegar mixture.

Put the cabbage into a large enough bowl for things to be mixed around and sprinkle the sesame seeds over the top. Pour on the dressing, mix everything together and then crunch the noodles over the top. If you felt like crumbling some peanuts over the top as well as some coriander (cilantro) leaves, do.

Tomato and spring onion
Serves 2

SALAD | 250 g (9 oz) best-flavoured tomatoes
bunch of spring onions (scallions), chopped
Pret seasoning (Basics, page 251)
2 tbsp olive oil
1 tbsp balsamic vinegar

SLICE, QUARTER OR HALVE the tomatoes, depending on their size, and place them in a shallow bowl. (By putting them in a shallow bowl, more tomato pieces will remain in contact with the dressing than if there is just a puddle of it in the depths of a high-sided thing.)

Scatter the spring onion over the tomato and season. Pour the oil over first, followed by the vinegar. It is even possible to make this salad without vinegar at all, the acidity of the tomatoes mixes with the oil to a perfect balance. By adding balsamic vinegar you are increasing the sweetness and giving an extra dimension — so it is worth it, but certainly not essential.

If you were to find a source of particularly well-flavoured chives, they could be substituted for the spring onions. So often these days chives taste of absolutely nothing, but growing your own might well produce spectacular and pleasing results. If that is the case, use lots.

If using cherry tomatoes, you may be tempted not to cut them up at all because they look so pretty whole. Whilst the look is certainly compromised by halving them, the flavour is enhanced dramatically. The dressing combines with the juice and seeds and everyone benefits.

★ THE LUNCH BOX ★ THE LUNCH BOX ★ THE LUNCH BOX

Cucumber and dill
Serves 2

SALAD | 1 cucumber, finely sliced or cut into sticks, peel on or off
1 tsp salt
1 tsp caster (superfine) sugar (optional)
1 tbsp chopped dill
2 tbsp crème fraîche
coarse-ground black pepper

PUT THE CUCUMBER into a bowl with the salt and sugar, add cold water to cover and leave for about an hour. This softens the cucumber, but there will still be a crunch.

Drain the cucumber in a strainer and rinse — in case it has too much salt lurking on individual pieces. Mix the dill with the crème fraîche and add lots of black pepper. Add to the cucumber and stir everything together. Chill and serve, either on its own or with cold chicken or salmon.

NOTE Using ridge cucumbers, rather than the usual ones, gives more flavour and a different texture — do try them.

Potato, broad bean and bacon — hot or cold
Serves 2

SALAD	8 boiled potatoes, cold, chopped roughly
	2 cloves garlic, crushed
	100 g (3½ oz) bacon lardons, fried or grilled until crisp
	100 g (3½ oz) broad beans, simmered until tender
	2 large sprigs rosemary leaves
	3 spring onions (scallions), finely chopped
	2 pickled cucumbers, finely chopped
	coarse-ground black pepper
FOR COLD	3 tbsp real mayo (Basics, page 236)
	6 drops Tabasco
FOR HOT	2 tbsp olive oil
	1 tbsp balsamic vinegar
	6 drops Tabasco

Making a potato salad can be something you set out to do from scratch, the sort of thing one might have a craving for early one (hungover?) morning. It is also a great thing to have up one's sleeve for a leftover type of day. A few boiled potatoes sitting sullenly in the fridge with no aim to their life can be transformed into heroes of the table in a few very easy steps. And they can be made into a hot salad as well as a cold one — hard to decide which route to take, both are so tempting, so the weather might help you to make the decision.

The quantities are really not important, as long as you season whatever you have well with dressing, so that it doesn't seem a half-hearted attempt at using leftovers.

THE POTATOES CAN BE USED with or without being peeled — the skin, especially on new potatoes, gives a nutty flavour. If serving the salad cold, simply assemble everything in a large bowl and mix the mayonnaise in well so that it coats all the ingredients. Leave to chill in the fridge for some time, so that the flavours have time to mingle.

To serve hot, simply heat the oil in a shallow frying pan and add the potato. Don't shuffle it about too much, just let it establish itself on the bottom of the pan so that it develops a crispy surface then, using a fish slice, delicately turn it all about to give another surface the chance to crispen. You may need to add some more oil. Don't cover with a lid because it will produce a steamy atmosphere — and nothing can crispen in humid surroundings. When the potatoes are good and hot, add the bacon and broad beans and heat them through.

Take off the heat and add the remaining ingredients. Mix the vinegar and Tabasco together, pour over the salad and gently combine — if you feel a little more moisture is needed, add further dashes of vinegar — with or without a little oil. The more floury the potatoes were to start with, the more dressing they will need because they will absorb it as soon as it is added. Adding more cucumber or spring onions would liven the texture too.

Beetroot, cauliflower and crème fraîche
Serves 2

SALAD | 250 g (9 oz) cooked beetroot — best baked in their skins then peeled
(certainly do not use pickled beetroot)
1 red onion, finely diced
100 ml (3½ fl oz) French dressing (Basics, page 245)
1 small cauliflower, broken into florets and cooked in a little water or stir-fried
1 tbsp chopped mint
150 g (5½ oz) crème fraîche or soft goat's cheese

THE BEETROOT COULD BE sliced in circles, or alternatively (which is more satisfying to eat) cut into large irregular chunks about the same size as the cauliflower pieces. Add the red onion and half the dressing to the beetroot and mix well. Add the remaining dressing to the cauliflower and mint and mix well. Rather than combining the two camps, which would turn everything a uniform red, keep them separate and arrange them artistically on a large platter, making the most of the contrasting colours. Serve with the crème fraîche or goat's cheese in a separate bowl.

Spinach, bacon and quail egg
Serves 2

SALAD | huge pile of baby spinach leaves
12 soft-boiled quail eggs, peeled (see Note)
1 handful sugar snap peas
150 g (5½ oz) bacon lardons, fried or grilled
1 handful chives or the green part of spring onions (scallions)
100 ml (3½ fl oz) French dressing (Basics, page 245) with ½ tsp ground nutmeg
added to the vinegar before mixing with the oil

COMBINE ALL THE INGREDIENTS but don't add the dressing until the very last minute — spinach wilts staggeringly fast.

NOTE Peeling a dozen quail eggs is not fun unless you have masochistic tendencies. It is particularly time-consuming and tricky if they really are soft-boiled, but the result is so spectacularly worth it when the yolk oozes gently over the spinach leaves and combines with the flavours of the dressing. It is possible to buy ready-peeled quail eggs in some supermarkets (and they are not even too expensive) but they will certainly be hard-boiled.

SUSHI

Sushi is neither as scary to eat nor as terrifying to make as some people might expect.

Two possible responses to the above statement: Some will think 'whatever!', close the book and fry up some fish fingers, while others might pause for a few seconds and think 'well that's an interesting prospect' and read on.

Sushi is only rice and fish. Admittedly raw fish and, it has to be said, sometimes some very peculiar specimens are considered edible but, smoked salmon is raw fish (sort of) and the texture of sushi fish is (should be) very similar. What many don't realise is that the Japanese (and Japan is where, you will probably know, the concept originated) cannot abide 'fishy' fish. They do everything to make sure that their sushi and sashimi (raw fish eaten on its own without a 'pad' of rice for it to sit on) has no smell whatsoever. It is so fresh that it could probably still wink at you — if it had its head on. This is why the phrase 'sashimi-grade fish' stands out proudly — it means that you can expect ultimate quality and freshness, with no dubious provenance. The fish will have been frozen — okay, so winking is less likely, the fish having done time at –20°C (–4°F), but it would have been winking as it climbed into the deep freeze — not only to keep it at peak condition but also to kill off the parasites that can live rather too contentedly in some fish. In fact, it is actually illegal to serve sushi or sashimi with fish that has not been frozen — apart from tuna, for which the problem doesn't exist.

All you need to make sushi at home is some sushi rice, which is very short-grained (rice-pudding rice does very well as a substitute and is distinctly cheaper — but don't tell anybody); some wasabi, the greeny–grey paste that tastes like horseradish on speed; soy sauce; flat sheets of dried seaweed called nori; pickled ginger (*gari*) to refresh the palate in between mouthfuls and a variety of toppings that really don't have to be raw fish (or any fish) at all. Purists might tell you otherwise, and they are ones to keep in the dark about pudding rice, but it is tremendous fun to combine all sorts of interesting textures of fish, meat and vegetables with rice as the base or wrap.

Some of the best combinations are below, but do try anything that springs to mind (especially with some raw fish) because you can have huge fun experimenting. One of the best ways of enjoying the adventure is to pack your lunch box — and everybody else's — with a range of different ingredients, plus rice and seaweed, to be assembled in any way and order that they choose:

★   Avocado, cucumber and chopped chives with just a tiny dab of real mayo (Basics, page 236).

★   Beef, very rare and very finely sliced with thin slivers of ginger and spring onion (scallion) and a touch of horseradish mayo (Basics, page 243).

★   Tuna, fried top and bottom for 2 seconds — literally — then finely sliced and marinated in sesame oil, soy sauce and chilli sauce or mirin.

★   Grilled chicken or tofu with lightly cooked fine green beans and a dab of salsa verde (Basics, page 244) or some teriyaki sauce.

★   Prawns (shrimp) and slices of fennel with dill and lemon-flavoured mayo.

★   Carrot sticks or juliennes (very very thin — about 1 mm / 1/32 in) and burdock root similarly cut (buy from Chinese supermarkets) and strips of shiitake mushrooms cooked for about 10 minutes in stock and then bundled together.

In each of the above suggestions, the presentation can be made in a number of ways. Either make a 'pad' or small brick of cooked and seasoned rice and put the other ingredients on top, with a strip of nori wrapping them securely in position, or place a sheet of nori on a flat surface (or a tea towel, which makes rolling it up easier). It is also possible to buy small mats made from strips of bamboo linked together with small pieces of string. You put the nori (seaweed) on the mat, spread the rice over the seaweed and put the other ingredients in a line across the centre. Sprinkle sesame seeds, white or black, over the ingredients for extra texture and flavour. Roll up and cut into slices. Serve with soy sauce and wasabi or make your own dips from a variety of dressings — even French dressing would be quite interesting.

⚔ PASSION FACT ⚔

Our sushi men — from Japan, but living here so that we can have
fresh deliveries every day — use their finely-honed skills to produce
the most Japanese sushi that is possible
so far from home. Ideally one should eat these delicacies
as soon as they are made. We have to refrigerate the sushi while it
waits for you — this is a pity because it is, without doubt, better at
room temperature. Were you able to restrain the urge to wolf it
down as soon as the till shuts and maybe even wait half an hour,
the difference would be *sugoii* (Japanese for 'awesome').

Sushi rice
For about 36 pieces of sushi

RICE | 225 g (8 oz) sushi rice
300 ml (10½ fl oz) cold water
3 tbsp rice vinegar (or wine vinegar at a pinch)
2 tsp sugar (an extra teaspoon if you only have wine vinegar)
½ tsp salt

RINSE THE RICE in cold water until the water is clear of the cloudy starch. Put the rice into a saucepan with a well-fitting lid and add the water, or enough to cover the rice by about 1 cm (½ in). Bring to the boil with the lid on and then turn down the heat to a gentle simmer — or you could put the pan into a 200°C (400°F/Gas 6) oven, which gives a more even, all-round heat. Cook for about 30 minutes — all the water should have been absorbed, but don't keep checking because you will lose the steam that has built up inside the saucepan.

When it is properly cooked, the surface of the rice will be level, neat and dry to look at. Try a grain or two of rice and, if it is still hard (shouldn't be, but these things do happen), you can salvage things at this point by adding some hot water (from the kettle, not the hot tap), slamming the lid back on and continuing the cooking for a little longer. If the opposite has happened and you find

a soggy heap of overcooked rice sitting stodgily in the pan, turn it into rice pudding — savoury or sweet — and start again for the sushi!

Remove the hot rice into a bowl — the Japanese use a wide-based wooden one, specifically for the purpose — and move it around a bit with a spoon. If you wet the spoon before putting it near the rice it might help prevent the rice from gripping tenaciously and sticking (sometimes forever — it's remarkably clingy stuff).

Mix the vinegar with the sugar and salt and pour it over the rice, mixing it in very lightly so that the flavour is absorbed evenly but you don't want to mix so vehemently that the rice grains become unidentifiable. Use the rice when it has cooled a little (so that it doesn't cook the raw fish with its heat) but not stone cold and certainly not refrigerated.

4.00PM

THE SURREPTITIOUS SNACK

SNACKING ON THE WAY

Line your pockets, handbag or back-pack with healthy odds and ends. A little snack strategically consumed before rampant hunger sets in might just prevent you from over-indulging at lunch or dinner … Fingers crossed?

THE WAY ★ SNACKING ON THE WAY ★ SNACKING ON THE WA

ANIS BISCUIT
Old fashioned Spanish biscuit to
be enjoyed with coffee or tea.
Delicious, classic & cool!
TA 80P / £1 83P

LEGITIMAS Y ACRE!

PRET
★
HAND COOKED CRISPS
Sweet Chilli

T
CRISPS
Peppe

PRET A MANGER
NUTTY
[NUT MIX]
LITTLE BAG FULL OF NUTS

PRET A MANGO
★
PRET A MANGO
MANGO
A LITTLE BAG FULL OF
DRIED MANGO

CHOCOLATE
MOOSE
new
19/08

CHOCOLATE
MOOSE
new
19/08

CHOCOLATE
MOOSE
new
19/08

CHOCOLATE
MOOSE
new

We all know that we ought not eat between meals. And yet it is often far more fun to crunch, munch or slurp non-meals (horrid word, meal). There is the decadence or naughtiness of doing something vaguely wrong; the instant, grab and tuck-in nature of a snack, plus the very fact that it is a small quantity (rather than a whole monotonous plateful) that all contribute to making snacks appealing.

In fact, it is perfectly possible to consume very healthy, energy-boosting morsels (even low in calories) to fill the space between more formal eating sessions. Thinking about the possibilities in advance and planning what you might allow yourself will give a sense of virtue instead of the usual feeling of shame or guilt that creeps insidiously upon one whilst hiding a torn chocolate bar wrapper or crumpled crisp bag in the depths of the handbag or pocket after the emergency top-up of a sugar-low. So, use pockets, handbags, desk drawers, bicycle baskets, briefcases and glove compartments (when have you ever seen a pair of gloves occupying that particular space in a car? Or briefs in a briefcase for that matter? Yes, briefs were letters, but not any more) in a positive way and fill them with Pret pick-me-ups or your own inventions based on our inventory.

I suppose that there are basically two types of snack. There is the carrot stick (not carrot *and* stick), celery stalk, green bean or broccoli branch and dip, an apple, a piece of cheese or slice of salami, and the handful of olives type smackerel that won't keep for longer than a few hours. And then there are the longer-term supplies (nuts, crisps, dried fruits, popcorn, oat bars, cakes and biscuits) that can lurk contentedly in dark corners until the moment(s) of need arise. Both categories should receive adequate and appropriate consideration — snacks should be taken seriously.

NUTS AND BOLTS

Nut munch

INGREDIENTS

75 g (2$\frac{1}{2}$ oz) golden syrup

1 tbsp vegetable oil

1 tbsp honey

100 g (3$\frac{1}{2}$ oz) rolled oats

50 g (1$\frac{3}{4}$ oz) almonds

50 g (1$\frac{3}{4}$ oz) desiccated coconut

40 g (1$\frac{1}{2}$ oz) pecans

25 g (1 oz) soft brown sugar

25 g (1 oz) coconut flakes

PREHEAT THE OVEN to 180°C (350°F/Gas 4). Gently heat the golden syrup, oil and honey until runny. Pour over all the other ingredients and mix well until everything is well coated.

Tip out onto a well-greased baking tray (or one lined with baking parchment) and pat down to about 3 cm (1$\frac{1}{4}$ in) all over. If it is too sticky, dampen the back of a wooden spoon and use that to flatten the mixture.

Bake for about 45 minutes, checking regularly to see that it is not burning on top. If it is beginning to catch slightly, rest a smallish piece of greaseproof paper lightly over the top of the area that is being affected as protection — but be sure not to clamp it down or steam will accumulate and everything will become rather sticky.

When an even golden colour has been achieved, or as near as possible, remove it from the oven. Once it has firmed up a little by cooling, turn it onto a wire rack. Make sure that the air can circulate well so that the munch stays dry, rather than getting steamy and therefore tacky. When cool enough to handle, break into chunky irregular shapes. Store in airtight bags or containers for up to 2 weeks.

PASSION FACT

Arriba! Our food team tasted samples from all over the world in search of the perfect honey. On Thursday 8 February 2002 at 2.25 pm, they found it. Now our honey comes from the Yucatan Peninsula in eastern Mexico, where the local bees spend lazy days hanging out by the sweet-scented Tachonal shrub. No wonder it's caused a bit of a buzz.

Vanilla-coated pumpkin seeds

INGREDIENTS

1 egg white
15 g (½ oz) golden syrup
1 tsp vanilla essence
400 g (14 oz) pumpkin seeds (pepitas)

PREHEAT THE OVEN to 110°C (225°F/Gas ½). Mix the egg white with the syrup and vanilla essence in a large bowl. Add the pumpkin seeds and mix well so that they are all coated with the glaze. Spread over a baking tray lined with baking parchment.

Put in the oven for about an hour, turning and shuffling the seeds every now and then so that they all get the chance to dry. They will stick together and that's fine — actually not just fine, it's what you want to happen so that you can eat them in crispy clusters.

Remove from the oven when the majority seem dry. They may brown a little but not necessarily. If you'd prefer them toasted, turn the oven up by a few degrees and leave them in for a further 5–10 minutes, but watch them keenly because they can burn very easily. Let them cool on the baking tray — it's hard to move them about when hot. When cold, gather the pumpkin seeds and store them in an airtight bag or tin.

Eat them as a snack, but they are also excellent to eat sprinkled over puddings, muesli and ice cream.

You could also gather together a selection of pumpkin seeds, sunflower seeds, sesame seeds, almonds, dried cherries and raisins — which is our combination in 'Nuts and bolts' — or the 'Cherries and berries' mixture of dried cherries, strawberries, cranberries and raisins. These are almost muesli, without the oats.

Pret muesli

INGREDIENTS

50 g (1¾ oz) dried fig, chopped

50 g (1¾ oz) dried mango, chopped

40 g (1½ oz) dried dates, chopped

40 g (1½ oz) roasted whole pecans

40 g (1½ oz) roasted whole almonds

20 g (¾ oz) dried cranberries, chopped

75 g (2½ oz) raisins

20 g (¾ oz) roasted flaked coconut

10 g (¼ oz) pumpkin seeds (pepitas)

50 g (1¾ oz) sunflower seeds

50 g (1¾ oz) linseeds

10 g (¼ oz) grapenuts

200 g (7 oz) rolled oats (jumbo size)

ASSEMBLE ALL THE INGREDIENTS in a large bowl and give them a thorough mixing.

Store in an airtight tin or a tightly closed bag to keep fresh and dry. It should last for a few weeks.

Julian was hugely excited about this recipe as it launched in the test shops. Enthusiasm was mixed within the food team and there was a fair amount of friendly banter about the chances of success. Perhaps some were not entirely convinced that customers would realise that they could ask for milk or yoghurt to eat the muesli in the office; others could envisage the hamster-feed grains spilling out of the Pret pots and over computer keyboards. Whatever it was, the idea has been banked for a rainier day. A great shame, because the combination really is delicious — it's the best muesli combination ever.

Vegetable crisps

INGREDIENTS

3 carrots, peeled and finely sliced
2 parsnips, peeled and finely sliced
6 small beetroots, peeled and finely sliced
1 celeriac, peeled and finely sliced
sunflower oil, lots, but see below
salt (and possibly pepper too)

KEEP ALL THE DIFFERENT veg separate because they will cook at varying rates. You could soak them in cold water which would remove some of the surface starch, but do make sure that you pat them (very) dry with tea towels or kitchen paper before frying or they will spatter dangerously when they hit the hot oil.

Heat the oil in a heavy saucepan (for safety, use a stable, solid pan — hot oil needs respect). Test the temperature by dropping a veg slice into the pan — there should be sizzling around the edges, but if it is too violent, then turn down the heat and wait a minute before trying again.

Fry the slices in small batches for about 4 minutes, or until the bubbling stops, which will indicate that all the water in them has evaporated and they can become crisp. If the oil is too hot they will begin to burn — but as so much depends on the starch/sugar content, each batch will cook slightly differently and you may find yourself altering the heat rather frantically. Just stay alert and under no circumstances leave the room until the oil is safely off the heat and out of the reach of small (or even large) people.

Drain the crisps on kitchen paper and sprinkle them with salt and possibly pepper before serving them. You could also add chopped herbs or a few shavings of fresh chilli and spring onion (scallion) for a sharp kick. It can be hard to make the flavouring stick to the surface of the crisps, but persevere by shaking them about (gently). Always make more than you think you need!

NOTE If making potato crisps, you will find that different potatoes produce different results — all to do with the starch and sugar content (obviously) and this changes as the potatoes mature. We have asked the advice of our crisp people (all our people are crisp, alert, sharp, etc, naturally, but these are the crisp, crisp ones who supply us with our bags of, yes, crisps) and they say that you should try to find 'Maris Piper' or 'Markies' if embarking on potato crisping.

Like potatoes, all the other root vegetables can be brilliantly successful as crisps. They only need a fine slicing and a deep-frying — both of which can be slightly off-putting because of the fears of not achieving thin enough slices or the worry of having great vats of hot oil about the place. But it really isn't all that scary. Try slicing, if you can, with an attachment on your food processor. If that's not possible then acquire a mandolin (which is the old-fashioned, pre-processor bit of kit, used most often in the past for preparing cucumbers for sandwiches or potatoes for pommes dauphinoises). For the frying fears, if you don't have a deep fat fryer, it might not be entirely necessary to fill pans to swimming pool levels with hot oil but instead to fry smaller batches at a time, in more shallow depths.

Popcorn

Popcorn is possibly one of the most more-ish foods around and perhaps this is why, when sitting on a cinema seat being gripped by action on the screen, you can consume a ludicrously large carton of popcorn without it even registering. Luckily popcorn is remarkably low in calories — if 'air' popped rather than popped in oil — and if it is covered only with the merest hint of salt, it is probably even healthy (not entirely sure how mere the salting needs to be to make that claim, but perhaps it's best not to know).

Anyway, popping corn is the easiest thing in the world to do. You could make a mint by buying a bag of corn kernels, popping them and then lurking round corners near cinemas doing a spot of adventurous trading. The mark-up is phenomenal (though not for Pret's popcorn, of course). So outrageous is it that one would imagine huge skill must be required to produce the stuff. But no, you simply need a saucepan (spacious) with a lid (see-through is rather fun), some dried corn kernels, a tablespoon of vegetable oil and then some salt or sugar or some melted honey, chocolate and butter mixture to coat the fluffy white fellows when still warm.

Put the oil in the saucepan and cover the entire base of the pan one kernel deep with corn. Cover the pan with the lid — this is done both to protect your eyes and to keep the kitchen tidy because those popped pieces can sure travel, speed and distance, and you won't want to spend time picking them off the floor (you'd miss the film).

As the heat increases, the popping begins, first the occasional lone pioneer thuds against the lid, then a rumble or drum-roll of followers and finally an out-and-out explosion as all the remaining pieces hurl themselves forward and upwards, turning from desiccated inedibles into white, light and fluffy snacks as they go.

Season the corn with either salt or sugar or, if you're feeling bold, try melting 50 g (1¾ oz) each of butter and chocolate and a tablespoon of honey and pour it over the corn, stirring and lifting the pieces swiftly so that they're all coated. Let it cool completely before bagging it and taking off to market.

Black pepper cashews

It is fairly obvious that nuts are oily — they are the source of a large proportion of our cooking fats. When nuts are heated they can become alarmingly hot as the oil in them heats and, in a way, they are frying internally. So, be extremely careful when playing around with them in the heat. To kick-start the release of the internal oil, it is good to use some external oil in the frying pan — not too much or everything will feel greasy.

Fry cashew nuts in a little oil (sunflower is good) in a shallow frying pan and then add lots of coarse-ground black pepper and some salt whilst they are still in the pan, shaking them around. Add a splash of balsamic vinegar if you feel like sharpening the flavour slightly. It will evaporate through the nuts and give them a wonderful savoury taste.

Don't be tempted to taste them until they have been off the heat for a good 5 minutes and have cooled a bit. Also don't worry if they seem soggy when they are still warm — that sogginess will disappear and they will crispen when cold.

You can treat all types of nuts in this way and even combine different varieties. For added interest you could add all sorts of spices or herbs to the mixtures whilst they are cooking. For example, throw in some fennel seeds or rosemary sprigs, or cook in chilli oil instead of plain oil. The possibilities are endless.

Once they are completely cold, bag the nuts, or put them in an airtight tin where they'll keep for a couple of weeks quite happily.

SKINNY DIPS

These are crudités by another name (dreamt up by Nick on a really good day). The point is that these raw (or par-boiled) vegetable sticks sit, charmingly bathing, waist-deep in whichever dip has been selected, adding colour and interest without compromising health or girth.

Choose any veg you like but bear in mind that it needs to stand strong to be a worthy dipper — fine green beans tend to bend and asparagus can also be a bit limp if it is cooked even 30 seconds too long. The best are carrots, cucumber, broccoli, celery, red, green, orange or yellow peppers (capsicums), and even courgette (zucchini) sticks.

Taramasalata

INGREDIENTS

1 clove garlic, roughly chopped

1 slice soft white bread, soaked in milk then squeezed dry

200 g (7 oz) smoked cod's roe, skin removed (not essential)

1–2 lemons, freshly squeezed

100 ml (3$\frac{1}{2}$ fl oz) olive oil (make sure it is not a bitter one)

PUT THE GARLIC and bread into a food processor. Turn on the machine for a brief time so that the bread is chopped or bashed about a bit. Add the cod's roe. The skin is very thick and sticky so it's probably best to keep it out of this recipe, but if a chunky taramasalata would be enjoyed, throw it in.

Blend the ingredients as well as you can — more a case of breaking everything down. Add the lemon juice and things will begin to go a little more smoothly. Add the oil in a slow and steady stream with the machine running. It is at this point that it all changes and becomes more taramasalata-like. Pale pink (not like the stuff you buy that has the dubious colour of babies' knitwear) and flecked with the grains of real roe. If necessary, add some more lemon juice to sharpen the flavour. No salt will be needed but you may like to grind a spot of black pepper over it when serving.

Artichoke dip

INGREDIENTS	450 g (1 lb) tin artichoke hearts, drained
	1 lemon, freshly squeezed
	salt and coarse-ground black pepper
	50 ml (2 fl oz) olive oil

IN THE FOOD PROCESSOR, blend together the artichoke hearts with lemon juice, salt and coarse-ground black pepper. Add the olive oil in a slow, steady stream. Check the seasoning and serve.

Humous

Take a 450 g (1 lb) tin of cooked chickpeas, drain them and put them and a small clove of garlic in the food processor. Blend for about 10 seconds, then add a tablespoon of balsamic or white wine vinegar, a decent pinch of ground cumin, 1/2 tablespoon creamed horseradish and 1/2 tablespoon olive oil. Blend again for a further 10 seconds. If you'd like the humous to be completely smooth, keep going for as long as you care to. If you'd prefer there to be a few chunky chickpeas lurking (albeit in a dishevelled state) then resist the temptation to blend for a second longer than entirely necessary — in fact, you could reverse the order of everything, leaving the addition of the chickpeas until last. Another great addition is some finely chopped coriander (cilantro) leaf — about a tablespoon. It gives an extra dimension to the flavour and the flecks of green are attractive in the otherwise yellowy–brown paste.

Keep refrigerated and use within a few days because it really doesn't keep well to anyone's advantage — it starts to go fizzy as the chickpeas ferment and the flavour becomes decidedly suspect, so you'll know if it is to be avoided.

To serve this dip — and others too — cut the top off a pepper (capsicum), red or orange are best in this case because of the colour combination, remove the seeds and fill with the humous. Stand the skinny dippers in the pepper with their heads sticking up above the parapet (cut them long enough for this to be a possibility) and hand round. This is the most perfect example of portable food — food on the move. It looks great, tastes excellent, works from every angle because even the transportation is uncomplicated (just put them in a box so that they stay upright) and, most important of all, there is no packaging to dispose of — just eat the bowl when the filling has been snaffled by the dippers and there won't be a shred of evidence.

Guacamole

It is important for our Team Members working in the kitchens that each process is uncomplicated and requires minimum handling. There is enough to do when assembling our wide range of goodies without imposing fancy, fiddly extras. For this reason, we examine every new idea from a logistics angle as well as whether or not the thing will taste half decent (actually, completely stunningly decent is the brief and the goal).

So, when Nick suggested adding guacamole to our range, there was a spot oaf discussion (gentlemanly and civilised, of course, but it was definitely a discussion) and Julian said 'it can't be done'. There was a tangible silence — the sort that makes everyone wish that they were somewhere (anywhere) else — and then Julian added, 'if you can prove to me that the Team Members won't be in tears over this, then I shall consider it' (possibly not his exact words, but that was the gist of it).

It was the following week when we all gathered, excited but nervous, to watch the next round. Nick had provided Julian with: 1. an apron, 2. a mixing bowl, 3. a spoon, 4. half an avocado, 5. a masher and 6. a tablespoon of sweet chilli sauce. Julian put on the apron and washed his hands (by the way, whilst on the subject of hand washing, did you know that all Team Members working in a

Pret kitchen wash their hands every 20 minutes? A pinger pings and everyone downs tools and heads for the washbasin).

Back to the guacamole: apron on, hands clean, Julian set to. With one swift manoeuvre (and a spoon) he whipped the stone out of the avocado. Next, using the same spoon, he scooped the avocado flesh into the bowl. We all, collectively, held our breath. Taking up the masher in one hand and the sweet chilli sauce in the other he brought them both into contact with the avocado flesh at the same time. With no more than three mashing flourishes the contents of the bowl became a luxurious green paste punctuated with red chilli flecks. Guacamole. We were impressed — and so was Julian. Nick's face was a picture of happiness (with just the tiniest smidgeon of relief).

There is but one proviso to flag here. The recipe above relies entirely (with no room for indulgence) on the avocado being at the peak of ripeness. A hard, unyielding fruit will not relinquish its stone, nor will it bend to a masher's whim. By all means chop the avocado and coat it with chilli sauce, but the dipping will suffer and perhaps in a situation like this the veg sticks should be combined with the mixture in a salad.

SNACKING ON THE WAY ★ SNACKING ON THE WAY ★ SNACKING

PRET POTS

Rhubarb compote

INGREDIENTS | 3 sticks rhubarb, diced
30 ml (1 fl oz) water
50 g (1¾ oz) caster (superfine) sugar, more if you prefer it to be sweeter
3 slices ginger, peeled

PUT EVERYTHING IN a saucepan and heat gently over a low heat until the sugar has melted and the rhubarb has started to release its liquid content. Turn up the heat and allow it to simmer for about 10 minutes, or until the rhubarb is soft. Add more sugar if necessary at this point, but be very careful indeed when checking the flavour because it will be exceptionally hot.

Allow to cool, then remove the ginger. Serve at the bottom of a little pot with yoghurt or crème fraîche on top.

Very berry compote

INGREDIENTS | 250 g (9 oz) mixed berries (blackberries, blackcurrants, raspberries, redcurrants, strawberries)
30 g (1 oz) sugar, or extra to taste
30 ml (1 fl oz) water
½ lemon, freshly squeezed

PUT EVERYTHING EXCEPT the lemon juice together in a saucepan and slowly heat to give the sugar time to dissolve. Increase the temperature and simmer for a few minutes until all the fruits have softened — but don't let them become completely disintegrated. Add more sugar at this point if you feel it needs it — taking great care when tasting because it will be extremely hot.

Allow the fruit to cool, add the lemon juice and stir gently, then spoon the mixture into the bottom of a small pot. Add yoghurt or crème fraîche on top.

We sell a range of rather useful, not to mention tasty and even healthy pots of various combinations on the theme of fruit compotes and yoghurt, granola, honey and yoghurt.

They are of course ridiculously easy to emulate. All you need are some suitable little pots (you could use great vats but there a certain charm in the *petits pots* image), some varieties of fruit — either compote or salad — and some really delicious yoghurt. We use a pretty healthy 4%-fat organic type. If you use something with even less fat then there tends to be a watery separation — which is unappealing — and it means that whatever you have in the bottom of your pot becomes diluted. You could go fatter of course and choose a really creamy yoghurt or even a crème fraîche mixed with a little cream — if you are wanting to bulk yourself out a bit.

NIGHT TIME

THE MIDNIGHT FEAST

TOO GOOD TO MOVE

Stay in and indulge in a spot of excess. Forget dieting and being good — just once in a while — and tuck in to piled-high perfection. It makes all the boring abstinence so much easier, knowing that every now and then you really can go wild.

GOOD TO MOVE ★ TOO GOOD TO MOVE ★ TOO GOOD TO MOV

TOO GOOD TO MOVE ★ TOO GOOD TO MOVE ★ TOO GOOD TO

The stuff of dreams. The sandwiches that need two hands and a large napkin tucked into your shirt collar. The sandwiches that we wish we could make for you but just can't because they need to be eaten hot and dripping with the fabulous ingredients that really don't (won't) last a minute beyond their just-cooked perfection.

So, we shall hope to give you the direction (somewhat pedantic and opinionated perhaps) to carry out perfect execution of these drool-worthy combinations. Do challenge the pedantry quietly and in your own home and substitute where you please — but could you at least try the ideas bite for bite just once, because you may be pleasantly surprised and feel a warm glow of magnanimity once tastings have begun.

In repetition of our fundamental philosophy, use the very best quality ingredients you can find — you won't need vast quantities and the savings made by buying second-rate stuff will be apparent with every mouthful. For the more frugal amongst you that might be a positive experience, but for others it would negate the very reason for making these magnificent treats.

These concoctions — or assemblies — are not necessarily constructed from luxurious or extravagant ingredients. Cotton-wool white bread and rashers of bacon can reach heights of voluptuousness as effectively as any fillet steak or lobster claw. The important things to consider are quantity (enough), quality (the best), perfect timing (yes, of course) and relaxed consumption (really?). The first three are pretty obvious and easy to address; it's the last point that may need a spot of attention. After all, how often do we eat as a side issue? This entire book is about food 'on the move'. Well, not this chapter. This is where you focus on every morsel and mouthful; not perched, but sitting (or lying) in the most comfortable spot you can find; not during a telephone conversation, writing an essay or watching a television programme, but contemplatively, either alone or — if you're lucky — with someone important to you and for whom there is equal delight in eating something glorious.

We're not talking about romance and shady lighting or even dressing for the occasion. What we're hoping to convey is the appreciation of textures and flavours in perfect combinations — as simple as you please, or complex if you prefer (but no need to go in for culinary gymnastics).

There is a danger that this is all beginning to sound a little too self-conscious and precious. Not the intention at all. Just saying that every once in a while, however rushed and hectic your life, think of food as a sensual part of living. Slow down, stand (or sit) still, use your hands or chopsticks (might be too slow?), because if you touch the food — or have to pick at it delicately and clamp it between two sticks of wood — you'll understand it and appreciate it in a different way. And eating should be as much about the actual experience as it is about sustenance.

BEST EVERS

Hot cos bun

This is an idea for an absolutely, indecently fabulous vegetarian concoction — and if you are not a vegetarian, don't be put off, you will be amazed by a voluptuousness not usually associated with denial (of meat).

The list of ingredients should be gathered and prepared and, if possible, combined (and eaten) when everything that has been cooked is still warm (the whole point about being too good to move), which means that the lettuce leaves will wilt and take on a completely different flavour from their usual perky salad-ness.

Start with either a focaccia or ciabatta bun (the first is probably best for flavour whilst the second has greater elasticity and flexibility for holding everything together), brushed with olive oil and garlic and grilled on the inside only, then filled (from bottom upwards) with:

1. Cos (romaine) lettuce: two whole leaves from the middle of the lettuce — one on the top and one at the bottom of the sandwich — big enough, and with a good flavour between the dark green of the outside of the lettuce and the paler yellow of the heart. They will wilt when they hit the heat of the grilled bun. They are meant to.

2. Portobello mushroom: stalk removed, baked in a hot (200°C/400°F/Gas 6) oven for about 15 minutes with a brushing of olive oil, some salt and fennel seeds.

3. Red pepper (capsicum): quartered and grilled, first, skin side up, for about 5 minutes to loosen the peel to lift it off and then about 7 minutes the other way up, dotted with olive oil, a sprinkling of salt and some finely chopped garlic.

4. Asparagus: two spears, sprinkled with a little oil (olive is good) and coarse sea salt then grilled and when cooked but still crisp, brushed with a few dabs of truffle oil (an optional hedonistic touch).

Having piled all these ingredients on top of each other and before adding the second lettuce leaf and the top half of the bun, you need to add a final flourish: a tablespoon of double (thick/heavy) cream, to which some salt and coarse-ground black pepper and a dash of balsamic vinegar have been added. This tastes remarkably like hollandaise sauce and could not be less complicated to achieve. The acidity of the vinegar causes the cream to curdle (put crudely) and set — it is one of the most exciting discoveries to be made in the kitchen and you will find yourself unlikely ever to embark upon making a hollandaise sauce ever again (as if you were doing it every week). Eat the whole thing without further ado.

The best bacon sandwich ever

Forgive us if we throw you into confusion by making suggestions that do not seem entirely in line with our preoccupation with healthy eating but, when it comes to bacon sarnies, there have to be exceptions — after all, life is to be enjoyed, even if it means that we are shortening it with that very enjoyment.

So, what constitutes the best bacon sandwich? You may even disagree with our assessment and if that is the case you will have to write and tell us — politely though, please.

1. Start with cotton wool. Yes, we know, Pret is renowned for its grainy brown loaves, but for this it is essential to have white, soft and fluffy bread — often known as cotton wool. It must be so fresh that you almost have to check that it is not still too warm and ideally it should be pre-sliced (thick or thin, we'll leave that to you). If you have to cut it yourself (oh dear, an un-cut loaf implies a bit of quality and goodness) then a doorstep-sized slice might well be best with the opportunity for copious quantities of bacon fat to be absorbed at the thicker end.

2. Next, the bacon. Well, a variety of sorts could be considered. Streaky or prime back? Smoked or green? Dry or maple cure? For meatiness choose back, but for the extra flavour that comes in the fat of any meat, streaky is your man. Smoked has an extra depth and is strongly recommended. Dry-cure bacons lose less moisture during cooking and there will be none of that unpleasant white oozing that tends to come out of the wetter varieties. Do cook it well. The fat (however much or little there is) should be crisp. Stretch the whole rasher out on a flat surface, having removed the rind, before grilling (yes grilling/broiling or baking in a hot oven, rather than

GOOD TO MOVE ★ TOO GOOD TO MOVE ★ TOO GOOD TO MOV

frying, to prevent a smoke- and fat-filled kitchen), using the back of a knife to stroke along the whole length of the fatty bit and pulling it to its full extent, whilst holding firmly on to one end — it will always shrink during cooking but this will help a bit.

3. More questions; should it be brown sauce or ketchup? Fried egg inside or not? Tomatoes or greenery added? Easy, yes to brown sauce and ketchup (or maybe ketchup with Lee and Perrins), yes to egg, no to anything with vitamin C (well, of course, you can if you like — it would taste delicious — and it starts to become slightly healthy).

4. Cook (grilling gets the fat hotter and crispier more quickly) as many rashers as you think you'd like — at least three, probably five or six. Fry the egg — in oil for crisper edges, butter for flavour — and be certain not to overcook the yolk because it really must (must) ooze out with the first bite. Have the slices of bread ready with a dollop of brown sauce splatted onto the bottom piece, whack the bacon on top followed by the egg as soon as it is ready, grind lots of black pepper coarsely over it and then clamp the second piece of bread in place.

5. Without even pausing to put the finished masterpiece onto a plate (this thing should not be 'served' or anything so effete) just attack it with a huge bite. A massive bite, so that you release the yolk from its boundaries and hit all the flavours running and at once. You will probably be standing for the first half of this sandwich but once the adrenalin has subsided, take a seat and enjoy the remainder slightly more slowly.

TOO GOOD TO MOVE ★ TOO GOOD TO MOVE ★ TOO GOOD TO

Superlative steak sandwich

What would be the ultimate in decadence? Piling high the most extravagant ingredients in quantity (lobster, foie gras, truffles, beef fillet, oysters and caviar) or this sandwich of perfectly cooked rib-eye (not the most expensive but the best flavour) with mushrooms for texture and caramelised onion for sweetness, rocket for freshness, creamed horseradish for kick and tomato for colour.

1. For each sandwich: two thick slices of the best sourdough or malted grain bread, rubbed on each side with garlic and olive oil, then grilled (broiled). Alternatively, a baguette would be excellent too.

2. Mix a spoonful of creamed horseradish with an equal quantity of crème fraîche. Mayonnaise in this particular sandwich would be less successful because it would melt and separate into an oily puddle on contact with the warm ingredients.

3. One large (about 2 cm/³/₄ in thick) rib-eye steak grilled for 3 minutes on each side and then left to rest for 10 minutes. You will know how you like steak to be cooked and by all means keep grilling for longer (or shorter). The resting period is really important as it gives the juices within the meat time to settle down and even out. There will still be some heat in the meat and it should not have cooled too wildly before being eaten, but if you are worried, lightly cover the steak with a piece of foil. Lightly because you don't want to enclose it and make it sweat, losing its wonderful surface crispy tan. If the meat has a lot of really delicious fat on the outside that wouldn't crispen effectively in the shortish grilling time, cut it off and dice it before cooking the steak. Sprinkle this extra fat with salt and pepper and put it in a really hot oven (under the grill it would spit and smoke dreadfully) for about 10 minutes. It can then be served within the sandwich for an extra thrill.

4. 50 g (1³/₄ oz) shiitake or enoki mushrooms, cooked in oil and garlic and balsamic vinegar until soft and squidgy and succulent.

5. 50 g (1³⁄₄ oz) sliced onion rings, frying them first in olive oil and then introducing a spoonful of balsamic vinegar and keeping the heat up, watching carefully that they don't carbonise, but caramelise and darken and possibly go a little crispy at the edges.

6. A handful of rocket (arugula) leaves, very lightly dressed in French dressing (Basics, page 245) just before stuffing them into the sandwich. They will wilt very soon after the full construction is in place, but they will still be green and the stalks will retain a slightly crisp frisson in the first few bites.

7. Five cherry tomatoes, halved and sprinkled with coarse sea salt. A handful of chives, kept long rather than chopping them, for balancing on the tomatoes.

8. Make sure that everything is seasoned well once cooked. Starting with a slice of toast on the bottom, pile everything on top — the order suggested can be changed — finishing with the long green chives and the second slice of toast (surprisingly).

This will not be easy to eat. Does it matter? If it does matter and you'd feel much happier being elegant, then slice the steak into strips and not only will the other ingredients stay in place with greater stability (they'll mingle in a more friendly way, rather than perching perilously on top of each other) but the sandwich will be easier to tackle without falling apart.

There are all sorts of things that could be thrown in or substituted — just bear in mind that you are aiming for the steak to stand proudly at the forefront in flavour and texture, everything else is mere supporting cast. Perhaps you'd prefer to make it a one-man show, and there would be nothing wrong with that at all.

Pork fillet and bacon

BAGUETTE
FILLING

½ baguette, cut in half lengthways and brushed with olive oil and crushed garlic
200 g (7 oz) pork tenderloin
coarse-ground black pepper
1 lemon, freshly squeezed
6 rashers smoked streaky bacon
3 sprigs fresh rosemary
1 tbsp crème fraîche
1 handful lamb's lettuce or rocket (arugula)

PREHEAT THE OVEN to 200°C (400°F/Gas 6). Slice the pork in half lengthways. Sprinkle pepper and lemon juice over the inside and then place two rashers of bacon and half of the rosemary leaves in between the two halves.

Put the halves back together again and then wrap, or rather wind, the remaining bacon around the complete piece of pork, tucking some more rosemary in between. The bacon helps keep the pork from drying out and it also gives an attractive pink layer in an otherwise grey piece of meat.

Put the meat into the oven and roast for about 20 minutes. The bacon on the outside should crispen a little, but don't leave it to go completely crackly because you don't want the meat inside to be overcooked.

Heat the baguette in the oven for 5 minutes whilst letting the meat rest. Just before taking the bread out of the oven, slice the pork into 5 mm (¼ in) pieces.

Open up the baguette when it is out of the oven and spoon some crème fraîche into the centre. Immediately add the meat, pour over any juices in the pan, add the leaves then close the baguette and tuck in.

Sausages with marmalade

BREAD	2 thick slices German rye or wholemeal bread
FILLING	2 pork sausages, cooked and still hot
	1 tbsp thick-cut orange marmalade
	a dash of wine vinegar
	1 tsp dijon mustard
	1 tbsp chopped flat-leaf parsley
	tomatoes and/or peppers (capsicums), (optional) (see below)

KEEP THE SAUSAGES WARM in the oven whilst melting the marmalade with the vinegar in a small saucepan — this is simply to thin down the marmalade to a more suitable consistency and to give it a slightly more savoury tang. Let it cool a little (jams and marmalades retain heat for quite a long time because of the high sugar content).

Spread a dab of mustard over one side of one slice of bread and, having sliced the sausages in half lengthways, put them across the bread. Add the chopped parsley to the marmalade sauce and pour it over the sausages. If using tomatoes and peppers, pile them on top and finally add the second slice of bread. Eat quite soon, but please be careful to make sure that the marmalade is not too burning hot.

This may sound weird but it is one of the great British breakfast combinations. Upgrade it to lunch or supper by adding extra ingredients like a salad of halved cherry tomatoes and some chopped spring onions (scallions), slices of red pepper (capsicum) cooked in olive oil until soft and fondant-like and some really creamy and garlicky mashed potatoes. Adding a crushed clove of garlic to the marmalade would be pretty exciting too.

Cod fillet with tomato and garlic mayo

BREAD | 2 slices brioche

FILLING | ½ clove garlic, crushed

1 tbsp real mayo (Basics, page 236)

2 cos (romaine) lettuce leaves, cut into ribbons

1 tbsp tomato chutney mixed with 1 tsp tomato paste (concentrated purée)

150 g (5½ oz) cod fillet, grilled (broiled)

coarse-ground black pepper

1 handful chives

MIX THE GARLIC WITH THE MAYO and then stir half of it with the lettuce ribbons to coat them with the sauce. Pile the lettuce onto a slice of the brioche, followed by the chutney and then the fish. Spread the remaining mayo over the fish, season with pepper and scatter the chives on top. Add the second slice of brioche and serve.

Fish finger and chip ciabatta

BREAD | 2 pieces ciabatta bread, toasted

FILLING | 1 tbsp real mayo (Basics, page 236), with 1 clove crushed garlic added (aioli)

a squirt of tomato ketchup

a chunky handful of oven-baked chips (fries)

1 tbsp mushy peas mixed with 1 tsp malt vinegar

3 grilled (broiled) fish fingers

SPREAD THE GARLIC MAYO over the bread, squirt a line of ketchup on one piece of bread. Line up the chips along the bottom. Spread the peas over them. Balance the fish fingers on top. Add the top piece of bread and serve.

Cheese and anchovy muffins

BREAD	1 English muffin, halved and toasted
FILLING	2 anchovy fillets, drained of their oil
	30 g (1 oz) unsalted butter
	100 g (3½ oz) best, strongest, most delicious cheddar, grated
	100 ml (3½ fl oz) stout or brown ale
	1 tsp cornflour (cornstarch) mixed with ½ tsp Coleman's mustard powder
	1 handful rocket (arugula) leaves

POUND THE ANCHOVY FILLETS with the butter so that they can then be spread across each half of the muffin. Put the cheese in a non-stick saucepan and heat gently.

Add one tbsp of the beer to the cornflour and mix well. Add the remaining beer to the melted cheese and stir. Give the cornflour, mustard and beer mixture a further stir before adding it to the saucepan and then continue stirring whilst it heats and thickens the cheese into a cohesive melted sauce. Without the cornflour, the cheese melts into its separate components of fat and protein — the cornflour stabilises it again.

Pile half the cheese sauce onto one muffin half, adding a layer of rocket leaves between two doses of cheese and finishing with more leaves. Slap the second muffin half on top and eat immediately.

Christmas sprout and chestnut

BREAD	2 slices of the best and freshest wholemeal bread
FILLING	150 g (5½ oz) brussels sprouts, the smaller they are, the sweeter the taste
	75 g (2½ oz) chestnuts, cooked and peeled
	30 g (1 oz) unsalted butter
	50 g (1¾ oz) smoked bacon lardons
	generous sprinkling of ground nutmeg
	2 tbsp balsamic vinegar
	2 tbsp single (whipping) cream or crème fraîche
	lots of coarse-ground black pepper

CHOP THE TOUGH STALK END off the sprouts and then slice them as finely as possible — that's a start, because they no longer look sproutish. Roughly chop the chestnuts.

Heat the butter in a frying pan and add the lardons. Fry until quite crispy but not too desiccated — you'll want a slight chewiness left in them.

Keeping the heat quite high, add the sprout leaflets and let them sizzle with the butter, bacon fat and lardons. After a minute give them a good stir and then let them settle again for a further minute of high heat attack. Throw in the chestnut pieces and the nutmeg and stir again. No long cooking though, you're nearly finished and you absolutely do not want to give any opportunity for overdoing anything (particularly the little brassicas). Add a tablespoon of water and stand back as it hits the pan, releasing a loud hissing noise. Watch the sprouts turn a vibrant shade of green. Next add the balsamic and stir everything about efficiently and with purpose — the purpose being to spin round the chestnuts, bacon and the green leaves to coat them in vinegar, not to cook for any longer than absolutely necessary.

Take off the heat — don't delay — pour on the cream and stir (not only to distribute the cream but also to release some of the heat so that the cooking is stopped). Taste to check the salt level (bacon salt may well be enough) and grind lots of black pepper everywhere. Pile the mixture onto a slice of bread and squish down with the second slice to hold everything in place. Have a glass of cold beer at the ready, hold your breath and take a bite. Can you admit to even the smallest feeling of relief and conversion? I really hope so.

For advanced sprout-eaters this sandwich will even taste delicious cold, but beginners, don't rush, just take it in easy and gradual stages. Vegetarians can leave out the bacon and add some pecans or pine nuts for texture.

Sprouts are much maligned characters. They are often objects of hatred, fuelled by the nightmare of having been forced in childhood to consume waterlogged and overcooked grey things — the only thing to cast a dampener on Christmas day. They can, however, be absolutely delicious and a sprout addict will consume them in vast quantity from the moment they hit the vegetable stands around October.

Last December there was a fair amount of discussion about the food miles associated with imported Christmas treats. Traditionally at that time of year we consume numerous delicacies that have travelled many miles by plane from hot climates (marginally better if shipped instead, but still entailing tank-loads of fuel). Julian was interviewed on the Today Programme on Radio 4 and was called to account on the use of imported ingredients at Pret during the winter months; enthusiasm and inspiration for the sprout sandwich were fired, in a quest to add to the range of locally grown produce an exciting and, more importantly, seasonal sandwich that might be looked forward to with keen anticipation. Those amongst you for whom sprouts are linked with the devil will not be inclined to celebrate with them. Please think again. If honest, you will admit that it is partly the overcooked cabbage connotation that kills any remote chance of success or appeal and partly the texture. By cutting them finely and cooking for the minimum time, sprouts are delicious — I promise.

SWEET SANDWICHES

Chocolate, raspberry and rocket

BREAD | 2 slices malted grain bread or a malted grain roll cut in half

FILLING | 50 g (1¾ oz) 70% plain chocolate (see Note)

½ tsp sugar

2 tbsp crème fraîche with a few drops of vanilla essence stirred in

1 handful fresh raspberries

1 handful rocket (arugula) leaves

1 tsp balsamic vinegar

MELT THE CHOCOLATE in a small saucepan over low heat with the sugar. Allow to cool considerably. Dollop half the crème fraîche on one slice of bread and then spoon the cooled melted chocolate over the top.

Sprinkle the raspberries over and then add the rocket leaves, followed by the balsamic vinegar (dripped onto the leaves) and the remaining crème fraîche. Add the second slice of bread

NOTE If you can, do try to find something called *plaisir miel* (from a delicatessen or chocolate shop), which is a mixture of chocolate and honey. Before you dismiss the concept out of hand in a rant, or a shrug of the shoulders, it is amazing and distinctly addictive as it combines the bitterness of chocolate with a perfect balance of sweetness from the honey at the same time as being the most perfect consistency for spreading (or dipping one's finger into the jar) without the worry of having to melt chocolate.

Lemon curd, mint and mango

BREAD	1 brioche roll
FILLING	2 tbsp lemon curd (see recipe on page 210)
	5 or 6 mint leaves
	1 small mango, sliced
	coarse-ground black pepper
	1 tbsp sour cream mixed with a trickle of sweet chilli sauce

CUT THE BRIOCHE in half, remove some of the inside (to make space for enough filling — brioche are quite small in surface area! You might prefer to use slices from a brioche loaf if you enjoy a really chunky and full sandwich).

Spread the bottom half of the brioche with the lemon curd. Lay the mint leaves haphazardly over the curd with some bits sticking out at the side so that the green can be seen. Position the mango slices on top and grind some pepper over them.

Roughly spread the sour cream over the mango and add the top piece of brioche.

It occurred to us that there really had to be a couple of sweet sandwiches in this book. After all, we have meat sandwiches for carnivores and vegetable sandwiches for health fiends so why not a little something for those obsessed with chocolate and a spot of sweetness — there is no rule (only experience) that dictates savoury domination in the sandwich world.

ANYTIME

THE BAKING DAY

HOME SWEET HOME

Although you would be right to give this chapter a wide berth because the cakes and bars are far too delicious, consider the fact that by making these at home you are avoiding all the 'nasties' that would be in so many bought examples. See, so easy to justify!

BAKING ....page **204**

HOME SWEET HOME ★ HOME SWEET HOME ★ HOME SWEET

After a long day, energy depleted (completely vanished), spirits low and potential irascibility high, you drag yourself through the front door, kick off your shoes, drop your coat/bag/child and collapse on the nearest horizontal surface (might be the floor if things are really bad). What you need is one of our cakes or slices or bars. Probably the Love Bar — that might set things straight (almost) or perhaps a brownie or even a fairy (godmother) cake. Not all of them or spirits will descend even lower about 10 minutes later when reality dawns and calories are totted up, but a small bite of each might be a good idea (variety being the spice, etc) — with a cup of tea, which is often referred to as a 'nice' cup of tea. Whether this refers to its character or the possibility that un-nice ones exist, not sure. But, in this end-of-a-long-day situation, definitely choose a 'nice' one.

Cakes are treats. Cakes are not eaten by mistake. They are not fuel in the everyday sense, more high-octane or embellishment when a biscuit (cookie) simply won't do. Pret cakes and bars are made from the basic good ingredients that should come in a DIY kit with every new home — eggs, flour (or oats), sugar and usually, but not always, butter. Additional ingredients, like chocolate, nuts, lemon juice, icing, whipped cream or strawberries are lily gilders — great to throw them in, but a cake can be a real cake without them.

Mothers used to have baking days. It's uncertain how many of those days (or those mothers) exist now, which is why Pret have stepped in and accumulated a ready supply

— in rather practical sizes and shapes we think, giving everyone the chance to select their favourite instead of one big round dictated flavour sitting in the middle of the table (or floor if that is where you have landed). By following the recipes in this chapter you can make a tray of each, cut them into sensible or fanciful shapes and freeze any that you don't need immediately. They'll thaw swiftly enough if you crave an emergency ration in a rush and will actually taste rather delicious when frozen.

Decorate your creations with flair and enthusiasm — you know the sort of thing, lots of pink sticky icing, little silver balls and hundreds and thousands to get stuck in the carpet (and remind you for months of your cake-eating sessions). Alternatively, opt for the ease of a gentle dusting with icing (confectioners') sugar through a tea strainer or small sieve. This looks instantly smart, understated, thoroughly laid-back and suave. Make sure that the strainer is completely dry to avoid the sugar sticking in lumpy clumps and rinse it jolly well afterwards or you will find that your tea tastes distinctly sweet for many cups. Another thing to bear in mind is to resist the temptation to wave your wrists with wild abandon when all you are wanting to decorate is the cake — icing sugar is really flighty when given even the remotest encouragement to waft beyond the intended target. And, finally, don't breathe in too deeply as you do your discreet waving — the fine white 'dust' can tickle your lungs and nose in a most uncomfortable way!

BAKING

TIPS FOR BAKING

Where we suggest chocolate chips, any chocolate can be substituted — it's just that chips melt particularly easily and evenly. The only thing to worry about is the quality of the chocolate — use the best you can find (which is usually the most expensive, unfortunately).

Butter is always recommended as unsalted because of the naturally more creamy flavour. If you only have salted butter and have no means of altering that fact, don't worry, of course it will be fine and nobody will notice. (Can't believe I have written that — I am so fussy about butter.)

If the recipe uses oil rather than butter, it is best to use a relatively light oil like corn or sunflower, but any bland vegetable oil is fine. Olive oil tends to be too heavy and strongly flavoured.

The size of baking trays and tins is given to try and help. Don't feel intimidated by these instructions. If your tins are not the same size, the recipes will still work just as well but you will need to adjust baking times to take account of the depth of mixture being cooked. If your tins are bigger your cakes will be flatter and will cook more quickly; if smaller, the opposite (obviously).

Unless otherwise specified, the quantities given are for a tray of cake 23 x 23 cm (9 x 9 in) — nearly (but not quite) a square foot of cake! How many slices or pieces you cut this into can be entirely your choice and whim.

PREPARING BAKING TINS

The older, darker and more beaten up a baking tin becomes, the better it is at doing its job and also at releasing the baked cake at the end. The metal becomes seasoned over use, the patina dull and black (which means that oven heat is absorbed rather than being reflected off what might once have been a shiny surface) and inevitably (as long as you don't wash them in a dishwasher) the build-up of oil and grease (sounds grim) makes it less likely that things will stick. But, it is still necessary to 'line' the tin before baking anything.

Lining can be done with a layer of baking paper or layers of oil/butter and a comprehensive dusting of flour or even sugar. The advantage of the paper is that it often adds a spot of extra protection from the oven's heat; the disadvantage is that it is difficult to fold the paper neatly enough to avoid crinkles or lines appearing on the cake surface and sometimes the cake mixture seeps between the folds, creating all sorts of origami-like complications that don't look wonderful once turned out and in full view.

Blueberry muffins
Makes 12

TOPPING	75 g (2½ oz) plain (all-purpose) flour
	25 g (1 oz) soft brown sugar
	50 g (1¾ oz) unsalted butter
MUFFIN	250 g (9 oz) unsalted butter, soft enough to beat
	200 g (7 oz) caster (superfine) sugar
	4 eggs and an extra yolk, lightly mixed
	250 g (9 oz) plain (all-purpose) flour
	2 tsp baking powder
	150 g (5½ oz) fresh blueberries
	a few drops of vanilla essence

PREHEAT THE OVEN to 190°C (375°F/Gas 5). Arrange 12 paper muffin cases on a baking tray. First make the topping by blending the ingredients together, either in a food processor or with the tips of your fingers — lightly and with minimum handling. It should become like crumble topping — clusters of crumbly dough.

To make the muffins, beat the butter and sugar until pale and fluffy. Gradually add the eggs, beating well between additions. Sift the baking powder and flour together into the mixture. Mix in gently and then add the blueberries and vanilla essence.

Fill the paper cases two-thirds full of the mixture and sprinkle some of the topping mix over each case. Bake for 20–25 minutes, or until the muffins are golden brown. These muffins are best eaten fresh and slightly warm.

NOTE The muffin part of this recipe can be used to make fairy (godmother) cakes — simply leave out the blueberries and decorate the tops, once baked, with pastel pink icing and some little silver balls or sprinkles.

Banana cake

CAKE
2 eggs

200 g (7 oz) soft brown sugar

300 g (10½ oz) banana, mashed with a fork

2 tsp bicarbonate of soda (baking soda)

¼ tsp salt

130 ml (4½ fl oz) vegetable oil

240 g (8½ oz) plain (all-purpose) flour

45 g (1½ oz) banana, chopped

ICING
30 g (1 oz) unsalted butter

225 g (8 oz) icing (confectioners') sugar

100 g (3½ oz) cream cheese

½ lemon, freshly squeezed

PREHEAT THE OVEN to 120°C (235°F/Gas ½). Grease a 20 cm (8 in) round baking tin. Whisk the eggs and sugar together until pale and fluffy. Add the mashed banana, bicarbonate of soda, salt and oil and continue mixing at a low speed until well combined. Sift the flour into the mixture, increase the speed gradually and keep going until no flour is visible. Fold in the chopped banana and put everything into the tin.

Bake for 1 hour, or until a skewer poked into the centre of the cake comes out clean (with no uncooked mixture clinging to it). Allow to cool in the tin for 10 minutes and then turn onto a wire rack to cool completely.

Make the icing by beating the butter and icing sugar together until pale — not easy with relatively little butter and you may have to add the cream cheese and lemon juice before becoming entirely successful in getting a frothy whipped concoction. Do this with the whisk at high speed. When light and airy, spread over the top of the cooled cake using a palette knife. Allow to set before cutting the cake.

⚜ PASSION FACT ⚜

Unlike an English rose, our apples can be on the ugly side.
At Pret we believe organic apples are good value. They taste better
than mass-produced fruit because they are harvested naturally.
They are not sprayed with pesticides, wax or other chemicals.
They are not kept in chillers for an eternity. Organic apples come
from small orchards and are picked by hand using an ancient
contraption called a ladder. They have blemishes and irregular
markings — like real apples should.

Apple cake

INGREDIENTS

4 eggs

250 g (9 oz) soft brown sugar

1 lemon, zest only

225 ml (7½ fl oz) vegetable oil

2 tsp ground cinnamon

¾ tsp baking powder

125 g (4½ oz) sultanas (golden raisins)

35 g (1¼ oz) rolled oats

275 g (9¾ oz) self-raising flour

400 g (14 oz) peeled and diced apple — bramley are best

50 g (1¾ oz) demerara sugar

PREHEAT THE OVEN to 165°C (320°F/Gas 3). Grease a 20 cm (8 in) round baking tin. Whisk together the eggs, soft brown sugar and lemon zest until pale and fluffy. Add the oil, cinnamon and baking powder, whisking at a low speed until well combined. Add the sultanas and oats and then sieve the flour into the mixture — mix well, still at a low speed and then give a quick burst at high speed to ensure that no flour lumps still exist.

Fold the apple chunks into the mixture and put everything into the baking tin. Sprinkle the demerara sugar over the surface and bake for about an hour — or until the trusty skewer, forced into the depths of the hot cake, comes out looking clean and without even the smallest sign of raw cake mixture. Allow to cool for a good 10 minutes in the tin before turning onto a wire rack to cool completely.

Lemon curd
Makes 450 g (1 lb)

INGREDIENTS	3 eggs
	3 lemons, juice and zest
	100 g (3½ oz) caster (superfine) sugar
	100 g (3½ oz) unsalted butter, very cold and cut in cubes

RIGHT. WHY MIGHT THIS GO WRONG? Well, you are dealing with eggs and heat, which can lead to disaster but doesn't have to. (An interesting point about eggs in lemon curd specifically is that sugar makes them set at a higher temperature than they would on their own, whilst lemon juice has the opposite effect.) But really the important things to concentrate on are:

★ Use a bowl that can be (safely) balanced above a saucepan of simmering water.

★ Keep stirring all the time.

★ Add the butter a cube at a time and make sure that it really is cold because it has a very useful role in lowering the temperature of the mixture.

★ If you feel that things may be heating too fast, add more butter or, in the case of real panic, take the bowl off the pan and put it on a cold surface (or even into a waiting bowl of iced water that you had prepared earlier) until the moment has passed.

★ Stop cooking as soon as you notice that the curd is beginning to thicken. The residual heat will continue the process.

So, to start, put the eggs into a bowl and beat them lightly with a fork to combine the yolks and whites. Add the lemon juice and lemon zest with the sugar and stir everything together well.

Position the bowl over a saucepan of simmering water and begin to stir with a wooden spoon, making sure that you are scooping over all areas of the bowl, base and sides. As the mixture begins to warm, add a cube of butter. Keep stirring. See how long it takes for the butter to melt. At this stage, probably a few minutes, which is good. Every few minutes, as the previous cube gives up as a solid and melts into its liquid state, add another cube. Keep stirring.

When things have warmed more, the butter will begin melting into the mixture more swiftly. It could take as long as 10 minutes for the curd to warm (seems longer when you have to keep stirring) but don't be tempted to speed things up because that is when things can go awry. If the egg cooks too fast, rather than setting calmly, the result will be lemon-and-sugar flavoured scrambled egg with melted butter sauce. Take it calmly and slowly because it really will set eventually and the result will be a wonderfully smooth, pretty yellow lemon curd. And, as mentioned above, take off the heat as soon as you detect that it is starting to thicken.

Strain the curd (to leave behind the lemon zest which can be too grainy) into a clean bowl and leave to cool. And there you are. Hope you feel jolly proud.

This lemon curd will keep for up to a week in the fridge. It can also be put into sterilised jars and sealed to prolong the keeping time (still in the fridge) by a few weeks, maybe a month.

This really isn't difficult (you just need to know why it might go wrong — and then it won't). The difference between home-made lemon curd and the stuff in jars is so staggering that once you've convinced yourself that you really can make it, you'll be unlikely to buy it ever again — and think of all those lemon curd, raspberry, crème fraîche and rocket (arugula) sandwiches in a malted grain roll (an idea from the previous chapter) or lemon meringue pie and Lemon drizzle cake (page 212) you'll be whipping up.

Lemon drizzle cake

CAKE	150 g (5½ oz) unsalted butter, soft enough to beat
	200 g (7 oz) soft brown sugar
	3 eggs and an extra yolk
	4 lemons, zest and juice
	2 tbsp poppy seeds
	300 g (10½ oz) self-raising flour
	1 tsp baking powder
	pinch of salt
DRIZZLE	1 tbsp caster (superfine) sugar
	½ lemon, freshly squeezed
	1 tbsp lemon curd (see recipe on page 210)
	1 tbsp sugar 'pearls' (they look like hailstones) or demerara sugar

PREHEAT THE OVEN to 180°C (350°F/Gas 4). Line a 20 cm (8 in) round baking tin with baking paper. Beat the butter and sugar together until light and creamy. In a separate bowl, lightly whip the egg and yolk. Incorporate the egg into the butter and sugar mixture, adding a small amount at a time. The mixture should become pale and delightfully fluffy.

Gently fold in the lemon zest and juice and the poppy seeds. Sift the flour and baking powder and salt into the mixing bowl and fold gently into the mixture — the best way to do this is by using a large metal spoon in repeated figure-of-eight patterns; sort of slicing down through the mixture, round the bottom and scooping in an upward slicing gesture, then down and round again, having turned the bowl a few degrees so that you are not covering old ground. This spreads the stuff about without bashing out the delicate air bubbles that have just been assiduously beaten in.

Pour the cake mixture into the baking tin and bake for 25–30 minutes, or until light brown on top. Turn onto a wire rack to cool.

Dissolve the sugar in the lemon juice. Drizzle over the cake. Spread the lemon curd on top and then sprinkle with the sugar pearls. Cut into slices. Keeps for a day or two in a cake tin or freezes well.

⚜ PASSION FACT ⚜

If you agree that our lemon cake is fantastic,
you've got Alan Miles to thank. Alan is the blacksmith who
invented and manufactured the huge metal grid which drizzles fresh
lemon juice on each and every slice we make. Pret cakes really
are handmade with superb natural ingredients; they always
have been and always will be.

Crimble crumble

BASE	125 g (4$\frac{1}{2}$ oz) unsalted butter
	60 g (2$\frac{1}{4}$ oz) golden syrup
	1 tbsp clear honey
	175 g (6 oz) rolled oats
	25 g (1 oz) soft brown sugar
	1 orange, zest only
	1 tbsp double (thick/heavy) cream
	450 g (1 lb) mincemeat (fruit mince)
	50 g (1$\frac{3}{4}$ oz) dried cranberries
TOPPING	150 g (5$\frac{1}{2}$ oz) plain (all-purpose) flour
	85 g (3 oz) semolina
	40 g (1$\frac{1}{2}$ oz) caster (superfine) sugar
	1 tsp ground cinnamon
	120 g (4$\frac{1}{4}$ oz) unsalted butter
DUSTING	30 g (1 oz) icing (confectioners') sugar

PREHEAT THE OVEN to 150°C (300°F/Gas 2). Grease a 23 cm (9 in) square baking tray.

For the base, melt the butter with the syrup and honey. Mix the oats, sugar, orange zest and cream together and then add the melted butter mixture, stirring well. Put into the baking tray and pat down and level with the back of a wooden spoon. Spread the mincemeat over the base and then sprinkle the cranberries on top.

Whizz all the topping ingredients very briefly in a food processor or rub the butter very lightly into the combined flour, semolina, caster sugar and cinnamon. Sprinkle the crumble topping over the mincemeat and cranberry surface. Bake for 35 minutes, or until light brown; a pale, shortbread appearance is ideal. Turn onto a wire rack to cool. Using a tea strainer or small sieve, dust with the icing sugar. Cut into squares when completely cold.

This is a variation on the theme of mince pies mixed with a crumble.

Pret bar

INGREDIENTS | 200 g (7 oz) unsalted butter

80 g (2¾ oz) golden syrup

40 g (1½ oz) clear honey

100 g (3½ oz) soft brown sugar

¼ tsp salt

90 g (3¼ oz) dried apple rings, roughly chopped

80 g (2¾ oz) dried apricots, roughly chopped

1 orange, zest only

25 g (1 oz) mixed candied peel

75 g (2½ oz) pumpkin seeds (pepitas)

30 g (1 oz) sesame seeds

350 g (12 oz) rolled oats

40 g (1½ oz) sultanas (golden raisins)

65 g (2¼ oz) dried cranberries

5 g (⅛ oz) poppy seeds

35 g (1¼ oz) sunflower seeds

70 g (2½ oz) dried coconut flakes

PREHEAT THE OVEN to 170°C (325°F/Gas 3). Grease a 23 cm (9 in) square baking tray. Melt the butter, golden syrup and honey in a saucepan over low heat. Mix all the other ingredients together in a large bowl. Add the melted butter mixture and stir everything together until well distributed.

Put into the prepared baking tray, pat down and level with the back of a dampened wooden spoon (prevents sticking) and bake for 20 minutes, or until just beginning to brown on top. Allow to cool slightly before cutting into slices or squares. The texture will harden when completely cold.

Love bar

FLAPJACK BASE	150 g (5½ oz) golden syrup
	1 tbsp clear honey
	200 g (7 oz) unsalted butter
	350 g (12 oz) rolled oats
	60 g (2¼ oz) soft brown sugar
TOPPING	60 g (2¼ oz) dark brown sugar
	130 ml (4½ fl oz) double (thick/heavy) cream
	60 g (2¼ oz) unsalted butter
	35 g (1¼ oz) pumpkin seeds (pepitas)
	45 g (1½ oz) dark chocolate chips
	35 g (1¼ oz) shelled pistachio nuts
	35 g (1¼ oz) chopped almonds

PREHEAT THE OVEN to 150°C (300°F/Gas 2). Grease a 23 cm (9 in) square baking tray. To make the base, warm the syrup, honey and butter until blended together in a large pan over low heat. Add the oats and soft brown sugar and mix well. Put into the baking tin and bake for 20 minutes, or until the surface is lightly browned but not dark. Then remove to a wire rack to cool completely.

Meanwhile, to make the topping, put the dark brown sugar and double cream in a heavy-based saucepan over low heat (this prevents the mixture from burning). Dissolve the sugar and then increase the heat and bring the mixture to the boil and keep boiling for about 5 minutes,

stirring continuously whilst the cream thickens as the liquid evaporates. The wider the base of the pan, the larger the surface area and therefore the quicker the evaporation. Keep an eye on the consistency and stop boiling before the cream catches and burns, but it needs to thicken so that it becomes a little like fudge.

Take off the heat and stir in the butter until it has all melted. Pour over the flapjack and spread with a palette knife. While still warm sprinkle over the pumpkin seeds, chocolate chips, pistachio nuts and almonds. Cut into slices when completely cold.

Pret choc bar

INGREDIENTS

250 g (9 oz) dark chocolate chips

200 g (7 oz) unsalted butter

100 g (3$\frac{1}{2}$ oz) golden syrup

350 g (12 oz) digestive biscuits (graham crackers)

100 g (3$\frac{1}{2}$ oz) sultanas (golden raisins)

200 g (7 oz) milk chocolate chips

GREASE A SQUARE BAKING TRAY about 23 cm (9 in). Melt the dark chocolate chips, butter and golden syrup in a saucepan over low heat. Put the biscuits into a plastic bag or wrap in a tea towel and whack with a rolling pin to crush them (great way to vent minor irritations). Some will become so smashed that they'll resemble sand, whilst others will remain pretty chunky — that's perfect and will give the ideal combination of textures when you bite into a slab — chocolate sand and biscuit chunks. Stir the biscuit bits and sultanas into the melted mixture.

Put everything into the baking tray and flatten to a smooth level with the back of a wooden spoon. (Dampen the spoon if it keeps sticking.) Allow to cool to room temperature. Melt the milk chocolate chips in a saucepan over a low heat or, if you are worried about the temperament of the melting chocolate (which can be naughty at times, particularly if there is a lot of moisture in the air) then melt them in a small bowl over a pan of hot water, which is safer because it won't become too hot. Pour over the crunch base. Spread to the edges with a spatula. Chill the mixture in the fridge before cutting into slices or squares.

⊰ PASSION FACT ⊱

The never-ending development of our Brownie
is typical of Pret. We've improved the recipe 34 times.
Each change is minuscule but detectable. John D. Hess said,
'A race horse that runs a mile a few seconds faster is worth
twice as much. That little extra proves to be the greatest value.'
Same with our Brownie we think.

Chocolate brownie

INGREDIENTS | 225 g (8 oz) unsalted butter
300 g (10½ oz) dark chocolate chips
3 eggs
½ tsp vanilla extract
275 g (9¾ oz) caster (superfine) sugar
135 g (4¾ oz) plain (all-purpose) flour
¼ tsp salt

PREHEAT THE OVEN to 160°C (315°F/Gas 2–3). Grease a 23 cm (9 in) square baking tray.

Melt the butter and two-thirds of the chocolate chips in a saucepan over low heat. The smaller the pieces of butter, the quicker they will melt and the overall temperature will not get too high. Don't let the mixture become too warm or you'll have to wait before adding it to the egg mixture (so that the eggs don't scramble on contact with the other ingredients, which would be a great pity!). Whisk the eggs, vanilla and sugar together. If the chocolate mix is cool enough (if you can dip your finger into it without gasping at all it should be okay) add it to the eggs and sugar and mix well.

Sift the flour and salt into the mixture and fold in until all flour whiteness has disappeared. Pour into the prepared tin and level. Sprinkle the remaining chocolate chips over the top. Bake for 20 minutes — the mixture should be set and firm on top but not completely cooked. Using a skewer to test the texture would only show you if it were seriously under-done because, in this case, you actually want the mixture to be sticking to the skewer when you remove the tray from the oven so that the brownies remain wonderfully gooey and soft when cold. They will continue to cook when out of the oven because of the stored heat in the mixture. Err on the side of too little cooking rather than the opposite; if they are completely soggy you might just have to serve them with cream or ice cream in a bowl with a spoon. Allow them to cool a little before cutting into shapes with a sharp knife and don't remove them from the tray until completely cold.

Pecan pie

PASTRY BASE | 100 g (3½ oz) unsalted butter, very cold, cut into small cubes
| 200 g (7 oz) plain (all-purpose) flour
| ¼ tsp salt
| 60 ml (2 fl oz) iced water
FILLING | 70 g (2½ oz) unsalted butter
| 135 g (4¾ oz) golden syrup
| 185 g (6½ oz) dark brown sugar
| 30 g (1 oz) plain (all-purpose) flour
| 10 g (¼ oz) cornflour (cornstarch)
| 2 eggs
| 100 g (3½ oz) chopped pecans
| 250 g (9 oz) pecan halves

PREHEAT THE OVEN to 200°C (400°F/Gas 6). Grease a 23 cm (9 in) square baking tray with sides no more than 4 cm (1½ in) high. Make the pastry, either by putting the first three ingredients into a food processor and whizzing them for about 10 seconds, adding half the water, whizzing again and, if necessary adding the rest of the water to create a more or less cohesive lump that can be patted together and then rolled out as pastry. The less water you can get away with the better — damp, claggy pastry will be grey and tough.

Alternatively, make the pastry by hand (rather satisfying) by rubbing the butter and flour (plus salt) between (cold) thumbs and forefingers until one is vaguely blended into the other and then helped along by the addition of the ice cold water (not all at once, but as needed, a dash at a time) and stirred very lightly with a knife into a flaky paste — not a smooth dough, which would indicate too much mixing. The rubbing technique is not hard to acquire, it just needs patience and a lightness of touch. Don't feel that you need to reach the 'breadcrumb' stage so often mentioned in recipes — unless the crumbs are large and chunky — a fine breadcrumb texture would indicate overworked ingredients. The whole point about pastry is that it should be very crumbly and 'sand-like' to eat and this is spoilt completely if the flour has any chance whatsoever of developing its gluten content. (Quite the opposite of bread making where gluten maturity and stretchiness is vital, hence kneading bread dough — with warm hands.)

Once made, the pastry should be put in the fridge (covered in cling film or a plastic bag so it doesn't dry out) to rest (de-stress) until needed, or for at least half an hour. Pastry can be made days/weeks in advance and even frozen in batches (pre-rolled or in a lump) ready to be hauled into action to impress at short notice.

Roll the pastry with light and even pressure to a thickness of about 3 mm ($^1/_8$ in) — dab a little flour here and there on the surface and the rolling pin to stop the pastry sticking. Don't be tempted to over-roll because the same gluten principles will apply. It is far better to leave things looking a little unkempt than to roll and roll to smooth (tough) perfection.

Line the base and sides of the baking tray with the pastry, pierce all over with the prongs of a fork, rest it again in the fridge and then bake for 10 minutes (you could put baking paper and dried beans or rice to weight the paper and stop any potential rising of the pastry —

this is not entirely necessary because any risen parts can be gently persuaded flat again when out of the oven). This stage of baking without a filling is known as 'baking blind' and it is done to prevent a raw or soggy base that is particularly likely when the filling is runny or very wet before being cooked.

Make the filling by warming the butter with the golden syrup and the sugar in a saucepan over low heat. Don't let it get too hot — just warm enough to melt everything together — or you'll have to wait too long before adding to the eggs (to avoid scrambled egg). Stir in the flour and cornflour. Lightly beat the eggs and pour the syrup mixture onto them, stirring well.

Sprinkle the chopped pecans over the pastry and pour the syrup and egg mixture on top. Arrange the pecan halves in as organised a way as you like on top.

Bake for 25 minutes, watching every now and then to see that the top doesn't burn too much. A little 'caught' nut flavour is rather good, carbonised is not. Allow to cool before cutting and serving — hot nuts (and sugar) burn the mouth very effectively.

Oat and fruit slice

INGREDIENTS

200 g (7 oz) unsalted butter

100 g (3½ oz) golden syrup

40 g (1½ oz) clear honey

175 g (6 oz) dried mixed fruit with candied peel

100 g (3½ oz) soft brown sugar

¼ tsp salt

50 g (1¾ oz) dates, pitted and chopped

60 g (2¼ oz) dried apricots, chopped

1 orange, zest only

30 g (1 oz) sesame seeds

350 g (12 oz) rolled oats

5 g (⅛ oz) linseeds

80 g (2¾ oz) sunflower seeds

PREHEAT THE OVEN to 170°C (325°F/Gas 3). Grease a 23 cm (9 in) square baking tray. Melt together the butter, syrup and honey in a saucepan over a low heat.

Combine all the other ingredients in a large bowl. Add the butter syrup mixture to this bowl and mix everything well. Put into baking tray and bake for about 20 minutes, or until lightly brown on top.

Allow to cool quite a bit so that everything sets but, after about 20 minutes, whilst still in the tin, use a sharp knife to cut into 'bars' or squares. Only turn out when completely cold.

⤐✦⤏ PASSION FACT ⤐✦⤏

Only Pret's oat and fruit slice is stirred by hand
with a four foot long oar. Strange as this may seem, we've found
that mechanical mixers turn the ingredients into a horrid pulp.
Hand mixing the ingredients adds a lot of work but greatly
improves the flavour. It is partly for this reason that the
texture and taste of the product is so good.

Chocolate goddess cake

ICING	30 ml (1 fl oz) hot water
	30 g (1 oz) unsweetened cocoa powder
	70 g (2½ oz) unsalted butter, at room temperature
	140 g (5 oz) icing (confectioners') sugar
CAKE	3 eggs
	200 g (7 oz) caster (superfine) sugar
	100 ml (3½ fl oz) vegetable oil
	100 ml (3½ fl oz) water
	100 g (3½ oz) good-quality dark chocolate, 70% cocoa solids, melted
	135 g (4¾ oz) plain (all-purpose) flour
	75 g (2½ oz) ground almonds
	55 g (2 oz) unsweetened cocoa powder
	1 tsp baking powder
	½ tsp bicarbonate of soda (baking soda)

TO MAKE THE ICING, mix the hot water with the cocoa powder to make a paste and allow to cool. Beat the butter until pale and fluffy — this can be quite difficult with a relatively small quantity and you may need to start adding the icing sugar sooner to increase the bulk. Keep adding the sugar a spoonful at a time, beating between additions. Add the cocoa paste and beat until it is well incorporated. Put the icing to one side — not in the fridge, or it will be too hard to spread neatly over the cake.

Preheat the oven to 180°C (350°F/Gas 4). Line a 21 cm (8¼ in) baking tin with baking paper.

In a large bowl, using an electric beater, whisk the eggs at high speed until doubled in volume. Add the sugar and continue beating until pale and fluffy. With the whisk still on high speed, add the oil in a slow, steady stream. Keep beating until the mixture holds the shape of any trail across the surface.

Pour the water delicately round the edge of the bowl and then the melted chocolate. Fold them both carefully into the mixture using a large metal spoon (it's easier to be careful with a metal spoon than a wooden one). Sift the flour, almonds, cocoa, baking powder and bicarbonate of soda together over the cake mixture and fold in with smooth, light gestures.

Put the mixture gently into the prepared cake tin. All the pleas for gentleness are because, having worked hard to produce a light, fluffy, air-filled combination of ingredients, you do not want to whack the air out again by being rough. The air will be key in getting the cake to rise when the heat of the oven kicks in. No magic, a fundamental scientific principle of heat causing air to rise and if there is no air, the result is a leaden pellet of cooked ingredients sitting heavily at the bottom of the cake tin.

Bake for 65–75 minutes, or until a skewer comes out clean when poked into the centre of the cake. If the top of the cake seems to be browning too much before the centre is ready, simply balance a piece of baking paper or foil across the top of the tin and it will protect the cake from burning.

Leave the cake to cool for 10–15 minutes before turning it out onto a wire rack. When it is completely cold, slice across horizontally and spread a third of the icing over the bottom half. Replace the top and decorate with the remaining icing.

Carrot cake

ICING	400 g (14 oz) icing (confectioners') sugar
	100 g (3½ oz) cream cheese
	50 g (1¾ oz) unsalted butter
CAKE	2 eggs
	200 g (7 oz) soft brown sugar
	150 ml (5 fl oz) corn, sunflower or vegetable oil
	200 g (7 oz) grated carrot
	50 g (1¾ oz) walnut or pecan pieces, roughly chopped
	75 g (2½ oz) diced pineapple, fresh or tinned, roughly chopped
	50 g (1¾ oz) desiccated coconut
	200 g (7 oz) plain (all-purpose) flour
	1 tsp ground cinnamon
	1 tsp bicarbonate of soda (baking soda)
	1 tsp salt

PREHEAT THE OVEN to 150°C (300°F/Gas 2). Line a 21 cm (8¼ in) baking tin with baking paper.

The icing needs to be prepared in advance so that it can be chilled before spreading over the cake, so make this first. Beat the cream cheese and butter together thoroughly — easiest with an electric whisk, but strong hand beating would also work. Add the icing sugar to the mixture in three equal batches, beating well between each addition. Put in the fridge to set.

In a large bowl, using an electric beater, whisk the eggs at high speed until doubled in volume. Add the sugar and continue beating until pale and fluffy. With the whisk still on high speed, add the oil in a slow steady stream. Keep beating until the mixture holds the shape of any trail across the surface.

Gently fold the carrot, walnut or pecan pieces, pineapple and coconut into the cake mixture with a metal spoon in a figure-of-eight technique. Sift the flour into the bowl with the cinnamon, bicarbonate of soda and salt, and fold them in gently too.

Transfer the mixture to the baking tin — again with care, so that the air you've taken care to whisk in isn't whacked out. Bake for 1 hour, or until a skewer comes out clean when poked into the centre of the cake. If the top of the cake seems to be browning too much before the centre is ready, balance a piece of baking paper or foil across the top of the tin and it will protect the cake from burning.

Leave the cake to cool for 10–15 minutes before turning it out onto a wire rack. When it is completely cold, slice the cake in half horizontally and spread a third of the cream cheese mixture over the bottom half. Put the top back on and cover the whole cake with the remaining icing. It doesn't need to be completely smooth — in fact you could design any surface pattern you like.

ALL THE TIME

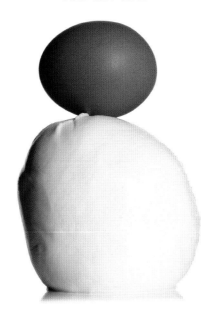

THE TOOL KIT

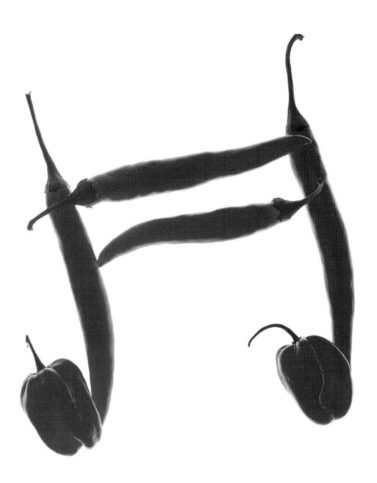

BASICS

Armed with these basic recipes you can take on the world. Mix a spot of this with a dollop of that. Stir up some secret combinations to impress — but do keep notes for the next time; it's so easy to forget where you began.

★ PRET A MANGER ★

★ BASICS ★ BASICS ★ BASICS ★ BASICS ★ BASIC

★ PRET ★

ASICS ★ BASICS ★ BASICS ★ BASICS ★ BASICS ★

MAYONNAISES

There's a real way to make real mayo and many books cover the topic. It is not difficult but it can be temperamental. The recipe that follows is dead easy and utterly reliable. It is also slightly lighter in texture than the 'real thing' because it has the egg white as well as the yolk in it. You can do all the same things to this as you would the other and it will remain more stable, so use it as your base for all the mayo combinations.

Mayonnaise is basically an emulsion, a sauce in which the particles of one ingredient are suspended in the particles of another. This will be permanent as long as it isn't heated — which is what makes it different from a blend or mixture, where the mingling is temporary but can be repeated as often as wanted (as in an oil and vinegar dressing). The idea is that you add oil to the egg and keep adding — it can hold absolutely masses, which is remarkable — until you get the consistency you want. Mayonnaise can be as thin as single (whipping) cream or almost as thick as butter (slight exaggeration) — it simply depends on how much oil you add. And it is possible, once made, to alter the consistency by adding more vinegar — which is often needed as a balance for the extreme oiliness.

By using a whole egg you give the whole enterprise a kick-start because the egg white is a much stronger, more amenable substance than the yolk, which is a bit precious and can easily throw a tantrum — in the form of curdling. Another way of adding stability in anticipation of disaster is to add a teaspoon of mustard powder at the beginning. It sort of keeps everything calm — strange for something of mustard heat. (Flour would work just as well but would taste horrid.)

Making mayonnaise uses a considerable quantity of oil — so to suggest that it is either healthy or slimming would be an over-statement! But it is a good way of adding moisture to what might otherwise be a dry collection of sandwich ingredients — and it beats butter for ease of spreading and adaptability of flavour.

Use a mixture of oils if you want to give a specific flavour to the sauce, but ideally, a light corn or sunflower oil is best. (Think hard before using large amounts of olive oil, because it is particularly heavy and has a strong taste that might intrude on the flavour of other ingredients.) Use white pepper if you don't want flecks to show, but it has a very different flavour from black.

Red wine vinegar could be used but the colour might make the mayo look murky, and balsamic would be unwise, both because of the colour and because it is rather more sweet than acidic — not quite right for cutting through the oil texture and taste.

Finally, on this fascinating topic, making mayonnaise by hand is a thoroughly satisfying, rewarding and self-congratulatory thing to do (when it works). It is, however, so much faster to make in a food processor that you might think about taking up alternative soul-improvers and give the machine a whirl.

Real mayo

INGREDIENTS

1 egg
salt and coarse-ground black pepper
1 tsp Colman's mustard powder
2 tbsp white wine vinegar
350 ml (12 fl oz) oil, more if you'd prefer a thicker consistency

PUT THE EGG INTO THE BOWL of the food processor with everything except the oil. Turn on the machine and, with it running, add the oil in a slow and steady stream.

Watch how the colour changes from yellow to pale yellow to almost white and listen carefully whilst pouring to how the sound changes as the mayonnaise begins to thicken. It has an almost 'hollow' sound once it is ready.

Check the seasoning and consistency, adding more salt and more vinegar if necessary (bearing in mind that the vinegar will make it more runny).

For the various mayonnaises we use in our sandwiches, some will have ingredients added at the end of the process, whilst others need to be started off with them in order that they blend to a sufficiently cohesive thing.

We are fanatical about mayo. You may well have noticed.
We insist on using fresh eggs (never dried or reconstituted)
and the best oil, but the real secret to great mayo is the
size of the bubbles after mixing. They should be tiny.
You are welcome to check ours with a microscope.

Yoghurt and mint mayo

INGREDIENTS | plain yoghurt (4% fat)
real mayo (see recipe on page 236)
mint, finely chopped
salt and coarse-ground black pepper

MIX TOGETHER EQUAL quantities of yoghurt and real mayo. Add 1 tablespoon of freshly chopped mint to every 200 ml (7 fl oz) of the mixture. Check the seasoning (because of the dilution with the yoghurt).

Fresh herb mayo

INGREDIENTS | real mayo (see recipe on page 236)
fresh herbs, finely chopped

ADD COPIOUS QUANTITIES of finely chopped fresh herbs to the real mayo. Depending on what it is to go with, choose (and mix) from tarragon (chicken); chervil (chicken and fish); thyme (cheese, beef, lamb, chicken); chives (egg, cheese, fish, chicken, vegetables); dill (fish, fennel, eggs); mint (beans, lamb, chicken, prawns); rosemary (meat, fish, vegetables).

★ BASICS ★ BASICS ★ BASICS ★ BASICS ★ BASIC

Caesar mayo

INGREDIENTS

1 egg

salt and coarse-ground black pepper

1 tsp Colman's mustard powder

2 tbsp white wine vinegar

50 g (1¾ oz) finely grated parmesan cheese

3 anchovy fillets, drained of any oil

1 clove garlic

350 ml (12 fl oz) oil, more if you'd prefer a thicker consistency

PUT THE EGG INTO THE BOWL of the food processor with everything except the oil. Turn on the machine and, with it running, add the oil in a slow and steady stream.

Watch how the colour changes from yellow to pale yellow to almost white and listen carefully whilst pouring to how the sound changes as the mayonnaise begins to thicken. It has an almost 'hollow' sound once it is ready. Check the seasoning and consistency, adding more salt and more vinegar if necessary (bearing in mind that the vinegar will make it more runny).

ASICS ★ BASICS ★ BASICS ★ BASICS ★ BASICS ★

⤜✠ PASSION FACT ✠⤝

Our tuna-man is obsessed with making only the most
perfect Pret tuna mayo. He mixes dolphin-friendly tuna
with Pret mayo, lemon juice and Pret seasoning, for exactly
20 seconds at 31 rpm. Never more. This is the only way to get the
texture just right — smooth, not mush, with a good 'tang'.

Tuna mayo

INGREDIENTS

200 g (7 oz) tinned tuna in brine or spring water, drained

½ red onion, finely chopped

1 tbsp creamed horseradish

1 tbsp lemon juice

1 tsp anchovy paste

1 tbsp capers, roughly chopped

salt and coarse-ground black pepper

100 ml (3½ fl oz) real mayo (see recipe on page 236)

MIX TOGETHER ALL the ingredients, except for the real mayo, in a bowl. When you've mixed it as thoroughly as you like it to be (you can leave it as chunky as you wish), stir through the real mayo.

Mustard mayo

INGREDIENTS | 1 egg
salt and coarse-ground black pepper
1 tbsp Colman's mustard powder
2 tbsp white wine vinegar
350 ml (12 fl oz) oil, more if you'd prefer a thicker consistency

PUT THE EGG INTO THE BOWL of the food processor with everything except the oil. Turn on the machine and, with it running, add the oil in a slow and steady stream.

Watch how the colour changes from yellow to pale yellow to almost white and listen carefully whilst pouring to how the sound changes as the mayonnaise begins to thicken. It has an almost 'hollow' sound once it is ready.

Check the seasoning and consistency, adding more salt and more vinegar if necessary (bearing in mind that the vinegar will make it more runny).

NOTE This recipe is based on the Real mayo recipe (see recipe on page 236), with the mustard powder increased from 1 teaspoon to 1 tablespoon.

Horseradish mayo

INGREDIENTS

1 tbsp grated horseradish
2 tbsp real mayo (see recipe on page 236)
salt and coarse-ground black pepper
whipped cream or crème fraîche (optional)

MIX THE HORSERADISH and real mayo together. Add salt and coarsely ground black pepper if needed. A little whipped cream or crème fraîche will make the sauce more luxurious (less 'everyday') and also lighter in texture. You may feel that the whole thing could be livened up further with a spot of vinegar; use white wine vinegar for a sharp boost or balsamic if you prefer the sweeter flavour. Be careful when adding vinegar to any cream — it will thicken it immediately, and too much will cause the sauce to curdle.

DRESSINGS

Salsa verde
(sounds more romantic than green sauce)

INGREDIENTS

1 slice brown or white bread

30 g (1 oz) capers

1 clove garlic

2 tsp dijon mustard

1 large handful baby spinach leaves

1 large handful flat-leaf parsley leaves

1 bunch basil

1 bunch mint

1–2 tbsp white wine vinegar

100 ml (3½ fl oz) olive oil

salt and coarse-ground black pepper

PUT THE BREAD INTO a food processor and blend to breadcrumbs. Add the capers, garlic and mustard, and blend. Break the leaves to get them into a more manageable bundle and pile them into the bowl of the food processor. Whizz everything together again. Add the vinegar and whizz again, then the oil and whizz once more. Taste and add more vinegar if necessary and season with salt and black pepper.

French dressing

INGREDIENTS

1 tbsp balsamic vinegar

1 tsp clear honey

1 tsp dijon mustard

1/2 lemon, freshly squeezed

1 clove garlic, roughly chopped

salt and coarse-ground black pepper

3 tbsp olive oil

MIX TOGETHER ALL the ingredients apart from the oil — this gives the flavours a better chance to mingle before they become coated with oil, which acts as a barrier. Add the oil and shake or whisk or stir frenetically. Taste and adjust seasoning if necessary, bearing in mind that it needs to have a decent strength of flavour if it is coating unseasoned foods and should be less strong if some of the salad ingredients are already salty (like anchovies, olives and some cheeses).

50:50 dressing

INGREDIENTS

plain yoghurt (4% fat)

real mayo (see recipe on page 236)

MIX TOGETHER EQUAL quantities of plain yoghurt and pre-prepared real mayo — what could be simpler? This dressing goes particularly well with chicken and seafood. Despite the worry that this might taste a little thin, you will actually be pleasantly surprised and might even enjoy the feeling of virtue associated with something rather healthy.

Sweet chilli dressing

INGREDIENTS

2 red chillies, finely chopped

1 clove garlic, crushed

2 red Asian shallots, finely chopped

1 tbsp fish sauce (nam pla)

1 tbsp mirin

1 tbsp wine or rice vinegar

squeeze of lemon juice

3 tbsp sunflower oil

COMBINE ALL THE INGREDIENTS TOGETHER except the oil. Mix well and leave to stand for about 30 minutes to allow the flavours to mingle. Add the sunflower oil and whisk well to combine before using. This dressing will keep for many weeks in the fridge.

Pesto

INGREDIENTS

20 g ($^{3}/_{4}$ oz) pine nuts

50 g (1$^{3}/_{4}$ oz) parmesan or pecorino cheese

30 g (1 oz) basil leaves

100 ml (3$^{1}/_{2}$ fl oz) olive oil

PUT THE PINE NUTS and cheese into a food processor and blend until smooth. Add the basil leaves and blend again. With the machine running, add the oil in a slow and steady stream. Check the seasoning of the pesto — it might not require any additional salt because the cheese may be salty enough already. Store in a clean jar in the fridge with the lid tightly closed. This pesto should last a good few weeks.

Pret yoghurt dressing

INGREDIENTS

1 green chilli, seeded

$^{1}/_{2}$ spring onion (scallion) (see Note)

$^{1}/_{2}$ clove garlic

1 tsp fenugreek seeds

$^{1}/_{2}$ lemon, freshly squeezed

2 tbsp plain yoghurt (4% fat)

salt and coarse-ground black pepper

BLEND ALL THE INGREDIENTS in a food processor, apart from the yoghurt and seasoning, until smooth. Stir the mixture into the yoghurt and season with salt and pepper.

NOTE You probably want the top half, but it doesn't really matter which you choose — the green part is more colourful and the white has a stronger flavour.

PICKLES AND OTHER BITS

Pret pickle

INGREDIENTS | 1 tbsp olive oil
1 large onion, diced
1 tsp ground ginger
10 g ($^1/_4$ oz) fresh ginger, peeled and finely chopped
2 cloves garlic, finely chopped
2 tsp tomato paste (concentrated purée)
50 g ($1^3/_4$ oz) sugar
450 g (1 lb) Bramley apples, peeled and cut into 1 cm ($^1/_2$ in) cubes
30 g (1 oz) raisins
100 ml ($3^1/_2$ fl oz) balsamic vinegar
200 ml (7 fl oz) water
salt and coarse-ground black pepper

HEAT THE OIL in a frying pan (that has a lid for use later on). Add the onion and cook over low heat, so it softens but doesn't brown. Add each of the ingredients, except the salt and pepper, giving time between the additions for the last one to be stirred and heated before adding the next.

Having added the water, bring everything to the boil and simmer over a low heat so the liquid reduces gradually and the ingredients can mingle for about 25 minutes. By balancing a lid over half the pan you will stop the spluttering of pickle juice over the cooker whilst still enabling the liquid to evaporate.

When the mixture is thick and dark (and before it catches on the bottom of the pan and burns), season it with salt and pepper and then bottle it in heat-sterilised jars.

Should you prefer a crunchier textured pickle, keep back some of the apple (and possibly some onion) to add towards the end of the cooking time, say for the last 10 minutes.

Slow roasted or semi-dried tomatoes

INGREDIENTS | tomatoes (your choice)
olive oil
salt and coarse-ground black pepper
thyme sprigs (optional)

QUARTER OR HALVE the tomatoes and place them on a baking tray, cut side up, with a sprinkling of olive oil, some salt and coarse-ground black pepper and possibly a few sprigs of thyme. Roast them in a 150°C (300°F/ Gas 2) oven for as long as possible — or until they are as dry as you would like them. It takes about 45 minutes for them to shrivel a little and for the flavour to concentrate wonderfully, but you could leave them longer and they'll become chewy. The better the flavour they had to begin with, the more exciting they'll taste when semi-dried, but it's pretty remarkable how good they can become even if they started as insipid, watery specimens.

They can be used to tremendous advantage in salads, on pasta dishes, on toast with melted cheese, on pizzas, on scrambled eggs, with steak and chips, even in sandwiches (and we do) … the list is endless.

Marinated chicken

INGREDIENTS
| |
2 boneless, skinless chicken breast fillets

2 tbsp white wine

5 drops angostura bitters

3 crushed juniper berries

2 thyme sprigs

1 tsp cider vinegar

2 bay leaves

salt and coarse-ground black pepper

PUT THE CHICKEN BREASTS in a shallow bowl. Mix all the other ingredients together and pour over the chicken. Marinate for at least an hour, turning the chicken every now and then to redistribute the marinade.

To cook the chicken, either sauté in a shallow pan for about 7 minutes (turning the chicken after half-time) or put the chicken breasts into a saucepan and cover with cold water. Bring to the boil and simmer for 10 minutes and then leave to cool in the liquid (which can now be called a 'stock' (sort of), to be used as a delicious base for a sauce or soup).

Chicken is completely delicious in sandwiches. Usually it is the breast (white) meat that is picked, probably because it looks neat and pure in colour. The only problem with chicken breast is that it can be extremely dry in texture (especially if it is overcooked). Do try to use thigh meat sometimes — it is cheaper, more succulent, harder to overcook and the flavour is excellent — alternatively marinate the chicken breasts before cooking, as we do (and no overcooking!).

Pret seasoning

INGREDIENTS

½ tbsp vegetable oil

2 tbsp each sea salt and coarse-ground black pepper

1 tbsp poppy seeds

2 tsp celery seeds

1 tsp mustard seeds

HEAT EVERYTHING in a frying pan over low heat for about 10 minutes, then allow to cool before putting in an airtight jar. Alternatively, you could store it in a flour shaker to make it easier to sprinkle into recipes.

We use our own home-made seasoning on all our sandwiches and in our salads. You may like to compose your own variation with different spices and possibly even a few very fine chilli flecks.

BREAD

Does anyone ever make their own bread? Julian thought not and in fact he looked faintly shocked by the idea. Disregarding bread machines — only because, like dishwashers and washing machines these modern conveniences save one from actually coming into contact with anything other than the ingredients at one end and the finished product at the other — bread-making is probably seen as something rather earthy and a little too wholesome for today's sophisticate. But, baking bread is possibly one of the easiest things to do in the world and is certainly one of the most satisfying — particularly when you feel like punching the living daylights out of someone. (Kneading bread dough should become part of all management training stress-handling strategies.) Not only will the exercise ease tension and furrowed brows, but it will also provide you with the healthiest, most natural, additive- and chemical-free loaves. (They will go stale far more quickly than a bought loaf — but doesn't that prove something rather significant?) 'Okay,' Julian agreed, 'let's include a recipe for bread.' So here it is.

The recipe to follow is for a rough malted grain type of bread that is mixed in one bowl, left to rise, pummelled for a while and thrown into a loaf (bar) tin (or made into individual rolls), left to rise and then baked. It is not a refined, cucumber sandwich type of loaf but it is delicious, simple and quick. Toasted, for use in a breakfast bacon and egg sandwich, it is sublime.

Home-made malted grain bread
Makes two loaves

INGREDIENTS | 1 kg (2 lb 4 oz) strong white bread flour, warmed in an airing cupboard
500 g (1 lb 2 oz) Granary flour, also warm
2 sachets (7 g/¼ oz each) instant, easy blend yeast
1 tbsp olive or sunflower oil
7 tsp salt (seems masses, but it does need it)
750 ml (26 fl oz) warm water

TOPPING | rosemary leaves, olives, walnuts, dried tomatoes, sesame or poppy seeds, one or all, used in any quantities you want (see Note)

PUT THE FLOURS IN A BOWL and sift in the sachets of yeast. Add the oil and salt to the warm water and pour it into the flour. Give it all a thorough mixing — using an electric machine (like a Kenwood or Kitchen Aid) takes the strain out of what is quite a weighty dough, but the machine needs to be made of strong stuff or it might complain. With only a lightweight hand-whisk available, a wooden spoon and elbow grease might be best. The beating (otherwise known as kneading, once everything has been combined and, if done by hand resembles a punching and folding routine) should go on until the dough becomes distinctly elastic and springy, so that if poked with a finger the dent produced springs back up again.

After 5 or 10 minutes of what is a remarkably therapeutic exercise, or when the desired springiness seems to be there, put the dough into a large, oiled bowl, sprinkle the top with a little flour and cover with a clean, dry tea towel (dish towel). The oil is to stop the dough from clinging to the bowl and the flour to prevent it from attaching itself to the towel. Leave the bowl sitting in a cosy and warm part of the kitchen or house (it could be the airing cupboard or even the bathroom — because a steamy atmosphere is ideal) and return to it about 30 minutes to 1 hour later. It should surprise you by being double the size. Bear this expansion in mind when selecting the bowl or you may find your airing cupboard enveloped by an amorphous doughy mass.

Preheat the oven to 180°C (350°F/Gas 4). When doubled in size, tip the dough out of the bowl onto a lightly floured surface. It will lose all of its light and airy structure and you will feel as though you have really hurt it. Don't worry, it will rise again. Do a little more pounding, but not much and then, either break off equal-sized pieces to make into roll shapes or put the whole lot into two 22 x 12 cm (8$^1/_2$ x 4$^1/_2$ in) oiled loaf tins. Leave the dough to rise again — it takes about 15 to 20 minutes, by which time the oven should be hot.

Bake for about 1 hour for loaves and 15 minutes for rolls. They are ready when knocking with your knuckles on the base of the loaf or roll produces a hollow sound. Take them out of the tins and cool them on a wire rack so that steam can escape and they won't go soggy.

With bread making — in complete contrast to pastry making — it is said that 'the wetter the dough, the better the dough', so don't worry if everything seems completely leaden and sticky at first. It should not be runny, but it certainly shouldn't be dry. It is quite staggering how much the absorbency levels of flour vary during the year or in different regions, depending entirely on the humidity in the air. You may think that you have had a really wet summer one year but the chances are that the occasional (seemingly frequent) showers will have had no impact on the general atmosphere and, as a result, a recipe that you have used confidently throughout the winter and spring

starts behaving in a strange and unpredictable way. If this happens, add some more water. Start with 50 ml (1$^3/_4$ fl oz) and if that isn't enough, keep adding in small quantities until you achieve the right consistency of dough. What is the right consistency? I have been trying to think of a suitable (appropriate and attractive) analogy but I think that the closest is not the most appealing. For a really good bread dough texture, think cellulited, un-toned flesh, barely contained within its skin — sorry!

A useful tip for the tedious washing-up stage of bread making: use cold rather than hot water for the initial rinsing of bowls, spoons and dough-hooks. If you start with hot water, the dough is cooked instantly and becomes strangely inseparable from the utensils, whilst with cold water everything is diluted and slips off without a fight.

NOTE The addition of extras can be made either after the second kneading (pounding) and before shaping the dough, or they can be scattered over the top of the loaves or rolls just before baking. Keep an eye on the toppings whilst baking because they will burn rather easily and may need to be covered (loosely) with a sheet of greaseproof paper or foil for protection halfway through the baking time.

STORE-CUPBOARD AND SUPPLIES

Having a store-cupboard (or larder or pantry — whatever you prefer to call it) of basics is invaluable. These are the things that lurk indefinitely — often improving with age, like worcestershire sauce — and provide an extra kick or dimension to whatever they are teamed with. It can be amusing every now and then to make a stock check, counting up the bottles and jars of repeat purchases sitting patiently at the back of the cupboard. How often does one stand at the supermarket checkout doing a silent roll-call (sometimes accompanied by moving lips) of store-cupboard supplies? 'Oil? Yes. Balsamic? Yes. Salt? Yes. Pepper? Yes. Tabasco? Tabasco? Did I or didn't I remember to get it last time? Yes, I'm sure I did. Or did I? No, don't think I did.' A quick turn to the person behind you in the queue, a muttered apology about just having to rush to the far end of the shop to get the one thing that you have forgotten, '... so sorry, do you mind awfully?' Then a break-neck dash to the Tabasco site — better buy two bottles so this doesn't happen again and anyway, it doesn't go off; hurtle back to your place in the line — probably grabbing some washing powder, tea bags and an oven glove *en route* (well, I don't know when I might be passing again). Get home to find, inevitably, that there are three bottles already (and although they are small, that's an awful lot of Bloody Marys to get through), and that what you didn't have was the Lea and Perrins. Again. Maybe you are scrupulously organised and this doesn't happen because you make lists … but I'd rather nobody checked my cupboard.

Some of these things might survive best in the fridge — particularly these days with 'best before dates' and 'refrigerate after opening' stamped over everything — so do remember to peer in there when seeking inspiration. In fact, look regularly, through all stashes of supplies — it's fun, revealing, sometimes embarrassing but the results can be magnificent because of the very nature of challenge and adventure without planning.

So, store-cupboard basics/essentials — here's a list to follow, with some clues about particular affinities. 'Peanut butter and jam/jelly' is a well-known combination; it doesn't appear here, but that does not invalidate the obvious (surprising?) pleasure it gives many people. If other favourites are missing, we can only apologise.

As far as fresh supplies are concerned, included are a few key points that we value in the selection process. Overall we ensure that we know precisely where and how all our ingredients are grown or reared and that they have as jolly an existence as is possible in whichever type of life they lead. We will always select home-grown rather than imported produce if we can, and make great efforts to support sustainable policies. Anything and everything you can do along these lines will inevitably help too — so thank you if you do so already.

ALMONDS. These nuts are jolly good for you. So many people realise this that, whereas originally Turkey grew the majority of the world's supplies, now vast swathes of the United States are being planted with almond trees (very pretty blossom in spring). The nuts are an excellent source of protein and fibre and they contain decent quantities of manganese and copper (not sure what the benefits are, but never mind). There is also a delicious Spanish variety which is shorter and rounder and possibly a more dense texture and sweeter flavour — they are called 'marcona' almonds. We use almonds in our Nut Munch, Love Bar, Granola and there is some in our chocolate cake. Add them to a salad or even in sandwiches for their texture and nuttiness — toasted particularly. Almonds are a useful substitute for (not just an addition but completely instead of) flour in cakes.

ANCHOVY. The essence or fillets can be added to salads, prawn sandwiches, dressings, potted shrimp, cheese toasties or wraps, cream cheese and celery sandwiches. Because of the saltiness, anchovy can replace salt in many things and will add a depth of flavour that isn't fishy at all — despite all expectations.

APPLES. We use most apples in our Apple Juice — rather than as a cooking ingredient (except for cakes and in Pret Pickle) — and our suppliers (Aspell) are fantastic at selecting the most appropriate, well-flavoured apple all year round from a seasonal apple calendar, blending from their range of apples that are stored as they are picked in a huge apple room (fantastic smell when you walk in). The apples are all grown in England and the varieties we use are Cox, Bramley, Russet and Discovery.

ARTICHOKES. We don't use artichokes in any of our sandwiches or salads at the moment, but that doesn't mean you can't — and you never know, we might suddenly spring to action with artichoke everywhere. Best to use the first, early, small artichokes if you can get them. Grill them whole or in slices and fling them into a salad or layer them with grilled aubergine (eggplant) in a hearty vegetarian sandwich. It is only as they mature that the choke develops and has to be removed to avoid serious damage to the tongue and throat. Interestingly, the flavour of artichoke does little to enhance the majority of white wines — best to drink red. Another idea is to make an artichoke dip by blending artichoke hearts (from a tin) with some garlic, olive oil, salt and pepper, a dash of vinegar and possibly a touch of cream (see recipe on page 168).

ASPARAGUS. It is not that the growing season has suddenly been extended but that we now (as a country) import asparagus from everywhere. Such a shame. It used to be a high point of early summer to spot the chunky stems of English-grown spears wrapped up in paper bearing the grower's name. It's still worth waiting for them to appear and to make the most of them (and their flavour) for the very few weeks that they are about. They don't need fancy treatment; wrap them in thin sleeves of streaky bacon (make the bacon wind around the stems so that the fatty bits are uppermost and have a chance to crispen) and grill (broil); or poke them into a salad having simmered them until just soft; or, best of all dip them (again, once cooked) in a simple mixture of cream, salt, pepper and a tablespoon of any vinegar — which will 'set' or 'curdle' the cream with its acidity and the whole thing will taste very similar to hollandaise sauce (without the effort).

AVOCADOS. Use Hass variety if at all possible. They are the ones we choose to use; and we only use them when they are at the peak of ripeness, having cosseted them with gentle warmth in our special ripening room and hand-turned them until they are really ready. Because of this attention to perfection, our team need only cut them in half and, using a spoon, flip out the stone. The same spoon is then used to loosen the flesh from the skin and the avocado is ready to be sliced or whatever the next hurdle might be.

BACON. We use the best (no phosphate), slow-cured, beech-smoked, streaky bacon — British whenever possible — from the belly of bacon pigs. We cook it fiercely so that it is really crisp and will stay crisp even after an hour in a sandwich.

BAKING POWDER. This is a chemical leavening agent made up of an alkali (usually bicarbonate of soda), an acid (cream of tartar, calcium phosphate or citric acid) and a starch to keep the whole compound dry and stable before use. Baking powder, unlike bicarb, is usually double-acting which means that it reacts first at room temperature and then again at higher temperatures (in the oven) which is jolly useful when baking. The addition of baking powder to a combination of 'creamed' butter and sugar has the effect of expanding the tiny and numerous air bubbles that have been whisked into the mixture and then, with the assistance of heat, lifting them, making a cake rise.

BASIL. We believe that the bold green colour, fantastically vibrant scent and the velvety feel as you bite into our big, fresh basil leaves combine to make a tremendous impact. Our Team Members painstakingly remove each leaf from its stalk by hand and we believe that the result (completely) justifies the effort.

BEEF. There are no beef sandwiches in our shops at the moment and this is really because, if we are going to put them in, we want them to be perfect and it is not easy to keep beef pink (with rarity — or perhaps it should be rareness) once it has been sliced. But, we are sure you will realise that if we did have beef in our range it would be the best ever. We would only look at grass-fed cattle, reared by kind farmers in lovely parts of the country (this country). They would have to be happy cows (until someone mentioned why they were there) with full pedigrees and family trees. And when it came to them no longer living in the fields (or anywhere else for that matter) we would ensure that their meat was properly hung (drawn and quartered) by expert butchers. Sorry, there should have been a warning at the beginning of this paragraph alerting vegetarians not to read this!

BICARBONATE OF SODA. Also known as sodium bicarbonate or baking soda. Apart from being useful (dissolved in water, to wash away unpleasant smells), when it is exposed to an acid it produces carbon dioxide and water. The carbon dioxide, which is a gas, rises when heated and it is for this reason that bicarb is used as a raising agent in cakes.

BREAD. Big topic: where do we start? We have our range — limited intentionally to avoid problems with quality control — which includes malted grain (low-fat, low-salt, slow-baked), white rye, bloomer, baguette (French flour, baked daily in our shops), artisan baguette (wonderfully 'nutty', dense and comforting — the newest to our range and it has taken off with great success; completely different to the other baguette and equally delicious), tortilla wrap (see 'Tortillas') and then the croissant and filled croissant range (French flour, traditional method, baked daily in our shops).

To make your own loaf is easy (see recipe on page 254). It won't have the same texture as the one we use, but it is tremendously rewarding (and very therapeutic) to make bread, so do have a go sometime.

BUTTER. In almost all situations this has to be (simply *has* to be) unsalted. Add your own salt by all means, but start with top-quality (unadulterated) wonderful, unsalted, creamy (French or Dutch are both fine) butter. Having said this, for some curious reason we actually think that 'President's Slightly Salted' version goes rather well in our Smoked Salmon sandwich — very strange.

CAPERS. These little unopened flower buds of a shrub are a 'love them or hate them' ingredient. If only we knew each day how many sandwiches to make with capers and how many without, life would be so much easier. But the same goes for tomatoes and onions and mayo and salt and mustard and meat and almost every other ingredient we use — some people are deliriously happy when we put them into a sandwich and others are really, really not. To those of you who are jolly disgruntled, we are very sorry indeed and hope you will forgive the fact that we aim to please lots of people as many times as possible — rather than all people every time. Capers are usually pickled in brine or vinegar, or are sometimes packed in salt, so they really should be rinsed before adding to a recipe. Caperberries are the fruit from the same shrub. They are completely different but as interesting in texture and flavour as the buds and can be thrown into the same recipes most successfully — sliced or roughly chopped.

CARAWAY SEED. This is great in white rye bread — it's what gives the bread the distinctive flavour. Caraway is also terrific in cabbage (raw or cooked), particularly savoy cabbage. Try a bubble and squeak sandwich next time you have some left-over cabbage and mashed potato and add some bacon or salt beef.

CARDAMOM. Pods or powdered — is used in Indian spice combinations (and often put in rice whilst cooking) but is also wonderful on its own with chicken or fish. It is often difficult to find the powder, so use the pods; split them and discard the pods, then crush the seeds by pounding them with a pestle and mortar. Cooking the powder in a little oil releases the flavour and removes the raw taste.

CHEESE. We use many different cheeses and we are rather fond of each of them; there is a wonderful Swedish cheese called greve which appears in many of our sandwiches. The closest approximation available in the UK is emmenthal or gruyère. The feta cheese we use actually comes from the Roquefort region of France. Mozzarella is authentic and traditional from Italy. We use parmesan — the proper stuff from Italy again — but when making something in our vegetarian range we use an Italian hard cheese that is set with vegetable rennet.

CHICKEN. 100% breast meat, no starch, phosphate free. Marinated in our special marinade (see recipe on page 250) then steamed or poached. Very healthy.

CHINESE RICE WINE. Also known as shao-hsing, is a little like sherry (see 'sherry' entry). Less good for swigging unless the quality is particularly high.

CINNAMON. This is a spice traditionally associated with apples (Pret Apple Cake) and Christmas (Pret Crimble Crumble topping). Use with savoury things too, particularly chutneys to go with lamb and in soups that need an extra boost.

CLOVES. As with cinnamon, cloves are associated with apple pie but are delicious with spicy (hot)

sauces for strong meats and game. Don't leave them whole in a sandwich filling because however delicious the flavour, if bitten on they numb the mouth — so effectively in fact, that dentists used to use them exclusively for toothache and pain relief before the days of anaesthetics.

CREAM OF TARTAR. This is an acid salt that among other things is used in baking powder and also on its own to help stabilise and add volume to beaten egg whites. (Vinegar would have the same effect on the egg whites but more would be needed and it would alter the proportion of liquid in the recipe too much.) Cream of tartar is naturally found in grapes and is a by-product in the sediment produced in wine making.

CUCUMBER. You may wonder why we don't make cucumber sandwiches at Pret. It was (almost) the first question I asked when I joined. I can't remember who said what or why but I have realised that it simply wouldn't be sensible. To make a really excellent cucumber sandwich — delicate, pale, crustless, with a yielding crunch and just the right amount of salt — is not really practical in the jostle and whirl of hearty eating in the heart of a city. They would be too effete, too precious, too silly really. But we do use huge numbers of cucumbers in other sandwiches, as you may have noticed, and we are very strict about the thickness of the slice or dimension of the stick (in the Skinny Dips or Hoisin Duck Wrap). We have a crafty attachment for our slicing machine that holds 5 or 6 cucumbers upright in a sort of canister so that they all hit the blade at the same angle — it's a lot of fun to watch. If you can find ridge cucumbers, do try them. They are about half the size but far crunchier than the usual ones and they have a wonderful flavour.

CURRY POWDER. A combination of spices pre-mixed for use in the kitchen. It can contain any or all of the following spices and more: cardamom, chilli, cinnamon, clove, coriander, cumin, ginger and turmeric. No self-respecting Indian chef would consider using something as generic and impersonal as a bought blend, but it can be very useful!

EGGS. Always free-range.

FENNEL SEED. Wonderful in salamis and Italian sausages or used in sweet–sour sauces with figs or dried apricots in a compote.

FISH SAUCE. Nam pla ('fish sauce' in Thai) is made from fermented anchovies and salt. Add it to fish, chicken, lettuce and prawns (shrimp) — it's very salty, so don't add sea salt too. Fish sauce is an excellent perk for soups that lack dimension. Don't breathe in the smell — it's truly horrid — the fishiness might well put you off, but you'll be pleasantly surprised by the effect that it has on the flavour of everything it is combined with.

GINGER, FRESH. Obviously not for the store-cupboard but keeps for ages in the fridge, and is particularly valuable with anything fishy (takes the fishiness away) and with Thai or Japanese flavours.

GINGER, GROUND. So utterly different from fresh ginger. It has a 'dustier' flavour that goes well with the strong tastes of garlic, chilli and onion, and in a marinade for sausages or spare ribs.

HAM. Ham should be dry (in other words, without water having been pumped into it as a way of increasing the weight); often the smoked varieties are driest, but there are many 'dry cured' un-smoked hams that are not soggy. Wiltshire cured ham is usually good.

Either use ham that has been very thinly sliced or, if cutting it yourself, make the slices really quite thick especially if you like the texture of meat. The flimsy texture of very fine (wafer thin) slices is delightful but not in a wodge; for the fluttery, tongue-tickling effect to be maintained, the slices need to be separated and strewn haphazardly over the bread. When cutting ham off the bone, the delight is in having all sorts of shapes and sizes; some with a bit of fat attached, some lean — it all contributes to the excitement of biting into the sandwich and not being entirely sure what you will find. As long as you can be sure that it isn't going to be gristle or anything really nasty, you can sink your teeth in happily and enjoy the experience fully. This is relevant to all meat- or fish-based sandwiches; be assiduous in taking the trouble to trim away veins, sinew, bits of bone and flabby skin (but, somewhat irrationally, if skin is excitingly crispy, throw it in not out). Many adults — and probably all children — are exceedingly put off by bits that really needn't be consumed and if they find them once in your sandwiches they will be wary forever. (It's the same for those horrible bits of apple core found in a crumble or apple purée — ghastly!)

Try ham sandwiches on malted grain bread with: Colman's mustard or wholegrain mustard mixed with a little mayo and some chopped chicory for its fresh crisp texture; radishes or watercress coated with olive oil and balsamic vinegar; mango and spring onion (scallion) marinated in lime juice and mirin; piccalilli and sliced new potatoes; cream cheese, cos (romaine) lettuce and olives.

HONEY. Ours comes from the Yucatan Penninsula in Mexico.

HORSERADISH. If you can find them, fresh roots of horseradish are simply amazing. Scarily strong when first cut into — and wear a gas mask (seriously) if you start grating it yourself — but the flavour diminishes rapidly once exposed to the air. Some brands of the stuff in jars are actually jolly strong too and particularly if they haven't been mixed with too much cream. They are the most sensible to buy and you can mix them about with cream or mayo or crème fraîche as you choose. We add a spot of horseradish to our Humous recipe — it has a remarkably good effect and very few people can guess that it is there. It is also a useful addition to sauces and gravies — adding an interesting extra note of complexity that doesn't actually jump out and scream 'ha ha, horseradish' but sits there quietly, adding tone and gravitas. (A little pretentious-sounding maybe, but do give it a try.)

HUMOUS. We make our own. You'll find the recipe on page 169.

JUNIPER BERRIES. One of the flavourings used for gin. We use them in our marinade for chicken (see page 250). Extremely good in a sugar syrup for dried fruits and for poaching cherries, figs and nectarines. Add a few to a pack of Pret 'Cherries and Berries' and poach them in water for 20 minutes before adding them to a winter fruit salad or to top a Pavlova with whipped cream and crème fraîche.

KETCHUP. It has to be Heinz.

LEMON. To make it easier to extract the most juice possible from a lemon about to be squeezed, roll the lemon about a bit between your hands or along a hard surface. This will help break down the interconnecting pith, making the juice run more freely with less squishing effort required from you. And, the lemons with thin skins tend to be juicier than thicker skinned varieties.

LENTILS. Use Puy lentils if possible. They retain their shape and texture even after lengthy cooking and they are rather a delightful shade of dusky green. They are an excellent addition to a wintery salad — with broad beans, mushrooms and lardons and a sharp lemon and coriander (cilantro) dressing.

LETTUCE. Choose a lettuce with flavour — real green flavour — and some texture. By far the most exciting are cos (romaine), unless you are in a foreign market where you will find all sorts of wonderfully muddy, insect-inhabited, really real salad leaves.

MARMALADE. The chewy bitterness of thick cut orange peel is wonderful with sausages at breakfast, in an All Day Breakfast sandwich or in a deliciously hot Bangers and Mash Wrap. Also great with duck and strong cheeses like the Spanish manchego.

MARMITE. The pots are truly adorable (particularly the tiniest one) and the spread is capable of inspiring passionate words from the most unlikely people. Add it to toasted soldiers; baked potatoes; hot pitta bread and melting unsalted butter; roasted carrots and parsnips; soups; a thermos of hot water; cheese on toast; mushrooms on toast, etc.

MAYONNAISE. Make your own (see recipe on page 236) or buy one of the better supermarkets' freshly-made own brand. The stuff in jars is perfectly okay, but will always taste like the stuff in jars.

MIRIN. Sweet and very slightly sour or musty (it's made from fermented sake, when it's the real thing) — add it to chilli or sharp things to soften a little.

MISO PASTE. Quite apart from its inevitable success as a soup base, miso is delicious, excellent and (coincidentally) healthy as a marinade ingredient for chicken, beef or fish. It happens to have a perfect consistency for clinging to whatever protein you care to bathe in its salty/nutty/sweetish depths. Available in different strengths of saltiness and sweetness (the palest, 'shiro', being the sweetest). Try lots and decide on a favourite. Miso keeps forever in the fridge — if any mould appears on the surface, scrape it away, it will only be because of contamination from a spoon dipped in last use and won't have affected below.

MIXED SALAD LEAVES. A selection of different plants, chosen for their colour, texture, flavour and how well they balance with each other. Washed in natural fruit extracts, no chlorine, no nasties.

MUSTARD, DIJON. This one is terrific with all sorts of cheeses, meats, cabbage and celeriac.

MUSTARD, ENGLISH. A British institution. And it has to be Colman's. Essential in a ham sandwich and pretty indispensable in melted cheesy mixtures.

MUSTARD, FRENCH'S. The all-American mustard introduced in 1904, which apparently was the same year that hot dogs were introduced in the United States — and they have been partners ever since. We use French's in our hot salt beef wrap.

MUSTARD, WHOLEGRAIN. Mix with mayo to use as a dip or combine with honey and sesame oil to make a marinade for chicken or sausages.

NUTS. See the separate entries on 'almonds' and 'walnuts'.

OIL, OLIVE. Olive oil used only to be available from a chemist (pharmacy) for medicinal purposes and it came in bottles of about 50 ml (1$3/4$ fl oz)! Nowadays we consume it by the litre and we pour it cheerily into and over absolutely everything. It is purported to be good for us (I'm very glad about that) and as long as we remember that it is fat in liquid form, with as many calories, we can continue to use it until someone discovers (and broadcasts loudly) a reason not to.

Olive oil is so readily available that it is now often the oil of choice for almost everything. In fact, it is not ideal for frying as it burns at a lower temperature than many other oils. However, it is particularly perfect for dressings. Each region and producer adds specific characteristics, as in grape growing and wine production. Sample lots of oils from different countries and regions until you find the one you like best.

OIL, SESAME. This oil goes particularly well with chilli, honey and vinegar for serving with chicken.

OIL, TRUFFLE. Truffle oil is most often found blended with olive oil because not only would it be too strong on its own, but it would also be hideously expensive. The deliciously earthy and rather exciting aroma can be detected from across a (crowded) room and one can suddenly crave a taste of it. Often used to great effect on pasta (with freshly grated parmesan) it would also be exceptional in a prosciutto and rocket (arugula) sandwich.

OIL, WALNUT. Really delightfully nutty and goes very well with grated carrot — not the obvious choice for a sandwich filling, but you never know. Must be kept in the fridge or it will lose its flavour very fast.

OLIVES. Ours come from Morocco.

ONIONS. We use the red-skinned variety because they are mild and they look so attractive in our sandwiches. You need to avoid the really pungent onions when eating them raw, or they will quickly dominate and compromise all the other sandwich or salad ingredients.

PEANUT BUTTER. Although one should, without a doubt, be using only the sugar- and salt-free peanut butters available, it does seem such a dreadfully worthy and tasteless product and I would strongly recommend that you stick with the (naughty) nice one. Make a dressing for a chicken salad and add a teaspoon of peanut butter with a spot of chilli. Or spread a slice of fluffy white bread with pb and add shredded cos (romaine) lettuce, some finely chopped spring onions (scallions) and some left-over minced (ground) beef or chicken. Top with sweet chilli sauce and a second slice of bread.

PEPPER. Black pepper does not last indefinitely. It does however, last far longer if kept whole until it's used. Buying ready-ground pepper, therefore, is less impressive than grinding your own straight into or onto the food, but it can be very useful. Choose the coarse-ground every time — the other is no more than sneezing dust.

PETITS POIS (PEAS). The saying 'frozen are fresher than fresh' relates to peas. They are harvested and podded instantly, then frozen before the day is out. This means that the starch inside has no time to sit about thinking of developing. The texture and flavour of the peas once they are cooked (directly from frozen) is fantastic — light and fresh enough to pop and crackle in your mouth. So don't be ashamed of admitting to using frozen ones.

POPPY SEEDS. The crunch provided by these small black dots is fairly remarkable. They do get stuck in the gaps between teeth and can be a source of embarrassment when spotted in the mirror after an evening of smiling, but they do liven both the look and texture of otherwise blandly smooth foods. Sprinkle over mashed potato in a hot wrap or on top of the remnants of a soufflé before filling a sandwich. We use them in our Pret Seasoning and Lemon Drizzle Cake — to great effect, we like to think.

REDCURRANT JELLY. Goes so exceptionally delightfully well with lamb that it shouldn't be without it — but if you find the jelly too sweet, simply mix a little vinegar or lemon juice with it. Add a spoonful on top of some brie or camembert — melted in the oven and then served oozing, with a spoon (or a straw).

RICE VINEGAR. Anything that needs a mild vinegar — this is the man for the job. Such a useful thing to have around. Really, it is.

SAUCES AND DRESSINGS. If possible, make your own. See recipes on pages 244–247.

SAUSAGES. Makes huge sense to go for top of the range where sausages are concerned. There are some fairly ropey ones about and the price relates directly to how much meat is involved. Cheap bangers have very (really very) little actual meat inside the skins — it's all flavour, fat and fillers (breadcrumbs or rusk). What you are looking for are signs that shout out 99.9% pork (or beef or a mixture). There are some wonderful Italian varieties called 'paesano' (either *dolce* or *piccante*, which mean mild and spicy respectively), rough and unrefined in all senses and really worth eating.

SEASONING. We make our own mix of salt and pepper with a few tasty additions (see recipe on page 251).

SESAME SEEDS. White or black, they produce a very strong flavour for something so small. They are excellent with both savoury and sweet foods. Sprinkle on chicken or humous with a few finely sliced spring onions (scallions) in a sandwich. Toast them and add them to a dressing.

SHERRY. A bottle of dry sherry is so useful! Not only for the occasional (frequent) swig, but excellent for livening a cheesy sauce, some left-over pâté or a thermos of soup. Were you to pop a red chilli into the bottle for a month or two it would really kick some action into the soup.

SMOKED SALMON. Hot- and cold-smoked are two completely different products. One is cooked from hanging about in hot smoke, whilst the other remains raw but flavoured by lurking in cold smoke-filled rooms. For our Smoked Salmon and Gourmet Salmon sandwiches we use Scottish, traditionally (cold) smoked, cured with salt and demerara sugar, from low-density salmon farms in open water.

STAR ANISE. This delightfully aromatic spice is wonderful with duck, broad beans and lentils.

TABBOULEH. We use Israeli tabbouleh which is a little like mini-pasta pearls and is prepared in more or less the same way. If you can't find this, make our salad with the more traditional tabbouleh. This is made with burghul (bulgur) or cracked wheat, possibly the world's oldest processed food. The wheat is cooked to mush and then spread in the sun to dry (not much of that in England, thus it's mainly a Middle Eastern product we accept with gratitude). When crisp and dry it is broken down into small granules. To use, you simply reconstitute it by pouring boiling water or stock over it and leaving it to absorb the liquid. Obviously the flavour will all be in the liquid or further additions (the wheat is completely tasteless) and it is surprising how much one needs to add to make it exciting. Once enough oil (olive/sesame/walnut), acid — lots (lemon juice/lime juice/vinegar) — and other flavours like crushed garlic, chopped parsley, chopped coriander (cilantro), chopped mint, diced onions and/or tomatoes, salt and pepper have been stirred in and absorbed, it really is a delicious and thoroughly healthy salad. (Couscous or pearl barley are good alternatives if cracked wheat cannot be found — but, whilst couscous can be reconstituted like the wheat, barley needs to be cooked like rice, for much longer.)

TAMARIND. This popular Asian ingredient has a useful acidity for sauces — sort of lemony, but different. Add it to pork, chilli dressings, or use as a paste to boost a vegetarian mixture.

TOMATOES. Vine-ripened or not? Interesting question. There is no doubt that tomatoes vary hugely in flavour (and texture) through the year. We are well aware that during some months our tomatoes are rather less amusing than they ought to be. But we do our very best to find the most delicious ones available and when they are good, they are wonderful. When selecting for your supplies, the words 'vine-ripened' should imply that they are better (and probably rather more expensive) than the economy packs, but sadly it doesn't always follow and sometimes it may be better to substitute another ingredient — maybe some semi-dried tomatoes or red peppers (capsicums).

TORTILLAS. If you can get hold of corn tortillas, all the better, they have more flavour than purely wheat ones — although both are eaten in Mexico, wheat in the north and corn in the south. Freshen them a little by heating them briefly under the grill, on a barbecue (or on the radiator).

TUNA. Sustainable, dolphin-friendly, in brine rather than oil if tinned.

TURKEY. Can be a good (usually cheaper) alternative to chicken although it does have a coarser texture and (obviously) the flavour is different. But, don't ever be tempted to buy the packs that admit to re-forming the meat. Only buy proper, solid breast or leg (sounds a bit racy). We steam our turkey, which means no addition of fat and yet it stays succulent. Rather healthy.

VANILLA. Pod and bean are mainly used in sweet things — milky or creamy puddings and for flavouring cakes and Pret bars. It is worth spending the extra to have the real thing.

VEGEMITE. The Australian essential in place of Marmite. It has a different flavour but is just as addictive. You either love it or you don't. Spread on the freshest, softest white bread and butter, and cut into soldiers to dip into a soft-boiled egg. Add to soups and sauces for extra body.

VINEGARS. Balsamic vinegar took the culinary world by storm a number of years ago. It is debatable whether or not one should invest in the really expensive ancient stuff because the cheaper varieties are pretty delicious too, particularly when they are being added as a final flourish in an already complex mixture. What one would like to avoid are the balsamicos that have had sugar added.

WALNUTS. It is perfectly possible to substitute pecans for walnuts. They are not only more succulent but they have a less dusty and less bitter flavour (that happens to go well with blue cheese).

WASABI. Ours is very pure and very definitely not coloured. The result is a distinctly grey, rather than bright green product. The taste is anything but grey — it can blow your socks off if you happen, in all innocence, to put a generous dose into your mouth. It is usually fairly obvious when a dining companion has done this; there is little to no conversation for a hefty few minutes, much swigging of anything liquid and the tendency to steer rather clear of the wasabi for a little while. Try using it instead of mustard or horseradish with roast beef — quite fun.

WINE VINEGARS. These are far harsher in flavour than balsamic and if one has become rather used to the soft, sweetish flavour of those from Modena and other romantic Italian regions, the acidity of white or red wine vinegar comes as a bit of a sharp shock. But don't ignore them completely because for mayonnaise, hollandaise or béarnaise sauces they really are the best — the kick is needed.

WORCESTERSHIRE SAUCE. Lee and Perrins — as it's also known — is so versatile. Try it with the following — cheese, meat, avocado, fish, potatoes, figs, taramasalata, raspberries and pears. It is staggering just how many foods benefit from the acquaintance and coexistence with this sauce. If an idea crosses your mind, give it a go, it will probably prove to have been inspired and you won't remember a time when you didn't include it in a particular recipe.

YOGHURT. We use a lean and healthy 4% fat yoghurt. It mixes well with mayo to reduce calorie consumption and is remarkably delicious for something that is actually beneficial.

ACKNOWLEDGMENTS

The atmosphere throughout Pret A Manger, both at the Hudson's Place office and in the shops, is warm, friendly, professional and determined. Without exception, everybody I have encountered within the company has been delightful and I wish I could mention them all here.

Those with whom I have worked most closely have been the Commercial Team, whose tremendous enthusiasm, dedicated hard work and light-hearted banter are a treat to observe, and the dynamics of the weekly Food Meetings have been a high point of my time with Pret. Each individual contributes his or her skill, expertise or opinion with firm and polite tact, whilst the *frisson* of potential challenge from Julian — as he raises his eyebrows in disbelief or breaks into a broad grin of delight — can give the almost prosaic discussion of sandwich filling an electric charge of surprising intensity. Nothing is done in a pale or lacklustre way; everything matters and attention to detail is paramount; whatever they do is done really well and without compromise. 'Less is more' is an expression that Julian likes to use and my goodness, at Pret they do their 'less' brilliantly.

The Commercial Team is made up of the following people: Director — Simon Hargraves; Marketing — Jay Middleton, Anthony Eadon; Design — Katy Robins, Oscar Segovia; Food — Ian Watson, Nick Sandler, Richard Edney, Valerie Laurent; Logistics — Colin Menzies, Antonio Madrid; New Product Launch — Yumi Li; Technical — Anita Kinsey; Purchasing — Ann Azzopardi, Sophie Brocklehurst; Sustainability — Nicki Fisher, Edward Metcalfe. I should like to thank each one of them, as well as Nadia Cohen, Angela Castle, Tom Lambret, Bridget Watts, Debra Piergentili, Mary McKendry, Clive Schlee and so many Shop Managers and their teams for all they did to make the writing of this book not only possible, but also fun. Huge thanks also to Ivo Herries, Caspar Helmore and Edward Rice for their help at the recipe testing and tasting stages:

JANE LUNZER GIFFORD